Elmer Luke and David Karashima

MARCH WAS MADE OF YARN

Elmer Luke is a writer and editor who has worked in publishing houses in New York and Tokyo, with a range of authors including Tom Wicker, Haruki Murakami, Colleen McCullough, and Robert Whiting. He is adviser to the Read Japan project of The Nippon Foundation.

David Karashima is the manager of The Nippon Foundation's Read Japan program—a partnership among authors, translators, editors, publishers, and universities to facilitate the publication of Japanese literature in translation. He is the author of an award-winning novel in Japanese, and a widely published translator of contemporary Japanese fiction into English, among them works by Hitomi Kanehara, Taichi Yamada, and Yasutaka Tsutsui.

MARCH WAS MADE OF YARN

MARCH WAS MADE OF YARN

Reflections on the Japanese
Earthquake, Tsunami, and Nuclear Meltdown

Edited by Elmer Luke and
David Karashima

VINTAGE BOOKS
A DIVISION OF RANDOM HOUSE, INC.
NEW YORK

Library of Congress Cataloging-in-Publication Data
March was made of yarn : reflections on the Japanese earthquake, tsunami, and
nuclear meltdown / edited by David Karashima and Elmer Luke.
p. cm.
"A Vintage Books original."
ISBN 978-0-307-94886-1
1. Japanese literature—21st century—Translations into English.
2. Tohoku Earthquake and Tsunami, Japan, 2011—Literary collections.
3. Fukushima Nuclear Disaster, Japan, 2011—Literary collections.
I. Karashima, David James. II. Luke, Elmer. III. Title.
PL782.E1M29 2012
895.6'080358520512—dc23
2011050010

* Words *

Losing everything
We even lost our words
But words did not break
Were not washed from the depths
Of our individual hearts

Words put forth buds
From the earth beneath the rubble
With accents like old times
With cursive script
With halting meanings

Words grown old from overuse
Come alive again with our pain
Grow deep with our sadness
As if backed by silence
They grow toward new meanings

Shuntaro Tanikawa
Translated by Jeffrey Angles

CONTENTS

FOREWORD

Imagine, for a moment, that you know nothing of what is happening here, or what is to come. Imagine that this is all still in the yet-to-be, or never-was, and that this is all you have to go by: this random clip on YouTube—digital, of course, and hauntingly crude. A "home movie," it used to be called, back in those touching, innocent days when there were homes.

The title heading on the clip tells you that what you are watching is a scene at Sendai Airport. A "live feed," as it were. The original title, in Japanese, is there too, palimpsest *kanji*. The date attached to the footage is March 11, 2011.

Someone is holding the camcorder, or phone; you will never know who. Maybe it doesn't matter. For a good minute or so, the public scene is so calm, so indifferently banal—the wide-open, expansive mouth of the Sendai terminal, with its huge wall of glass designed to beckon the natural world in, populated by people standing and walking, apparently without urgency—that you think there must be some mistake: what you are watching is . . . nothing.

The view is fixed, passive. As if the camera itself, to begin with, has no idea that any possible subject, or object of interest, is even in the vicinity.

It is a sound first, a low and faint rumbling that has you fiddling with the volume control on your laptop, trying to adjust away what you assume to be artificial white noise, because, whatever its source, the sound is not particular or recognizable in a human sense.

The people visible on screen—travelers, commuters, the odd uniformed transportation worker—produce their own noise too, an absentminded hum. It takes a while for these two noises to meet, and then separate. The first distinguishing moment arrives when one person—then two, then five—turns his head as if to listen to some song he thinks he might remember, but otherwise didn't catch.

What song? We can only try to imagine.

The sound becomes a gathering roar. The roar grows louder and more imminent, pressing invisibly on the scene we're witnessing. And now the first small cries of alarm can be heard inside the great space. A woman wheeling a carry-on whirls around to face the huge window. Then others do the same, staring out at the cold white glare of the tarmac that, in the construction of all this, has been poured over every inch of green. In the upper corner of the screen, a father picks up his small child. A few people begin to run, disappearing out of frame. The camera moves to catch them; then, perhaps sensing something, it scurries back to the great glass wall, and freezes there in terror.

A wall of water is surging past the terminal. It is a meter high—then, very quickly, two—washing baggage carts, a boarding ladder, a yellow car along its path.

Inside the terminal, screams can be heard now, above nature's roar of destruction. People are running, though there is no place to go.

The footage does not so much end as stop.

The stories begin.

—John Burnham Schwartz
Brooklyn, New York

INTRODUCTION

March 11, 2011. An earthquake off the northeastern coast of Japan—magnitude 9.0, duration six minutes, type megathrust—unleashes a fifty-foot tsunami that within fifteen minutes slams its way ashore, surging inland six miles, crushing all in its path, and triggering the slow, relentless leak of radiation from first two, then three, then five nuclear power plants. In one's wildest imagination, this is beyond conceivable.

But this is just the beginning. The waves do not stop; they recede and rush back in without ceasing. Nor do the aftershocks, which are themselves rolling earthquakes of terrifying magnitude. Nor does the death toll, or the number of missing, or the danger from radiation, which seems to be controlled incrementally, until the meltdown begins. Nor does the overwhelming sense of loss and despair.

Life goes on, indifferently and pitilessly, but life is not the same, and life will have been reconsidered. Here, a wide-ranging selection of writers offer their response to this uncharted moment—significant for the double blow we have sustained from both nature and man—a portentous marker in modern human history. The pieces—nonfiction, fiction, including a *manga*, and poetry—with perspectives near and distant, reconceive the catastrophe, imagine a future and a past, interpret dreams, impel purpose, point blame, pray for hope. Specific in reference, universal in scope, these singular heartfelt contributions comprise an artistic record of this time.

Some of the pieces were written for this anthology, some were first published in literary magazines in Japan, all amid the initial horror and uncertainty immediately following the disaster when lives, seemingly secure and in forward motion, were in a matter of minutes altered, thrown off course, beyond repair. This theme is most evident for writers from Tohoku, in northeastern Japan, which bore the physical (let alone emotional) brunt of the disaster. But no writer from Tokyo—the uncomfortable middle ground—or, for that matter, elsewhere distant (and safe) went unaffected or untouched. Life might have seemed to go on, but not without evacuation packs, aftershocks, brown-outs, unwashed clothes, empty store shelves, worry about contamination, worry for young ones—and elder ones, and our future—as well as nightmares, depression, worst memories, and prayers.

In this anthology, Tohoku natives Hideo Furukawa and Kazumi Saeki draw upon the immediacy of family and locality, where history provides a sense of continuity, however tenuous it may be under the circumstances; while Natsuki Ikezawa, who himself spent weeks delivering emergency supplies in stricken areas, focuses on the unexpected scope of emotions of those who give care.

From Tokyo, Mieko Kawakami depicts poignantly, if painfully—in the story from which the title of this collection was taken—how an earthquake far away can change the terms of something as "simple" as pregnancy. Similarly, with Mitsuyo Kakuta, for whom the entire notions of intimacy and dependency are called into question.

Hiromi Kawakami, whose work represented here was the first literary piece to emerge in Japan from the stunned silence after March 11, revisits the story that launched her career eighteen years before—with a landscape physically and emotionally changed. Her "updated" story is accompanied with a postscript and the original story that the new work was adapted from.

Kazushige Abe takes us to a place where we are perhaps most reluctant to go—into the ocean and beneath the waves—in an ironically positive tale about the irrational obsession to prevail. And Tetsuya Akikawa, in a tale lined with bureaucratic obsession, suggests redemption where we least expect it.

From the greater distance of western Japan, Yoko Ogawa writes of repose—and our need for it. David Peace, who has returned to Tokyo after several years in England, inhabits the world of Ryūnosuke Akutagawa as he experiences the social trauma of the Great Kantō Earthquake of 1923. Barry Yourgrau, sitting at his desk in New York, connects fragments of the Japan of his imagination to create a dreamlike narrative of post–March 11 life. Meanwhile, Ryu Murakami seeks meaning—and hope—in the twigs from a felled eucalyptus tree that he has stuck into dirt.

In Yoko Tawada's "The Island of Eternal Life," a group of doctors gathers fireflies to harness for evening light as they seek a cure of radiation sickness, while in Shinji Ishii's "Lulu," translucent women descend each night to comfort children orphaned by the disaster.

Then, in a change of pace, the Brother & Sister Nishioka team have drawn a cautionary *manga* for the day, and the poets Shuntaro Tanikawa and J. D. McClatchy remind us, in the depth and breadth of their response, of the value of words, simply written, gently spoken.

The idea for this project took gradual shape as we traveled among Tokyo, Tohoku, London, and New York, watching from near and far as March 11 and its aftermath unfolded. A thought became a shared idea that was developed further as we shoveled debris into the back of trucks in Tohoku, as riots racked London, as storms struck the East Coast of the United States, as a heat wave hit Tokyo, as floods raged through Bangkok, even as the cleanup in northeastern Japan proceeded but radiation continued to leak. It has been that kind of year.

We wish to thank the writers who have seen through the thick haze of the moment to clarity to offer us these pieces. We thank the translators who responded with care and generosity to their tasks. We acknowledge our excellent editors—Lexy Bloom, at Vintage; Liz Foley, at Harvill Secker; and Kazuto Yamaguchi, at Kodansha—for their patronage, encouragement, and advocacy of this project on three continents. We wish to acknowledge the Read Japan program of The Nippon Foundation for its support of the publication of this anthology. Proceeds from the book will go to support charities that have been sparing no effort in helping to rebuild towns, homes, and individual lives in Tohoku.

—Elmer Luke, New York
David Karashima, Tokyo

MARCH WAS MADE OF YARN

THE ISLAND OF ETERNAL LIFE

Yoko Tawada

Translated by Margaret Mitsutani

The hand that reached out to take my passport froze in midair. The young blonde inspector's face hardened into a frown, her lips quivering slightly as if she were searching for something to say. I spoke first. "I know this is a Japanese passport, but I've been living in Germany for the past thirty years, and I've just come back from America. I haven't been to Japan since then." I wanted to add, "My passport couldn't possibly be radioactive. So stop treating me as if I were contaminated," but thought better of it. When I opened the passport to show her the page with my permanent residence permit stamp, she finally took it with nervous fingers.

I felt ashamed of trying to prove my innocence by insisting I hadn't been to Japan since *that* had happened. Back in 2011 the word *Japan* elicited sympathy, but since 2017 sympathy had changed to prejudice. If I got an EU passport I wouldn't need to think about Japan every time I crossed a national border, but somehow I couldn't bring myself to apply for one. It seemed strange even to me the way I hung on to my old passport just when having one had become such a bother.

I stared angrily at the sixteen-petal golden chrysanthemum on its red cover. For a slightly disturbing moment, I thought I saw seventeen petals, though the idea that it could be genetically deformed was obviously absurd.

The suitcase I'd checked in New York did not arrive in Berlin. I went to the Lost and Found, and while I was writing down the color and shape of the suitcase, together with my address in Berlin and other necessary information, something awful occurred to me. In downtown Manhattan I'd loaded up with Japanese food that wasn't available in Berlin, such as soba noodles made from mountain potato, fermented soybeans, seaweed in vinegar, and spicy fish roe, all of which I'd packed in my suitcase. If it was opened, those packages, covered with words in Japanese, would surely be confiscated as dangerous material and sent to a Radioactive Waste Management Facility. The fermented soybeans might even be mistaken for peanuts that had undergone some rapid mutation due to radiation.

Since 2015, when direct information from Japan was cut off, rumors and myths had been multiplying like maggots, which had hatched into flies now winging their way across the world. Because planes no longer flew to Japan, it was impossible to go there and see what was actually happening. I'd heard that one Chinese airline was planning to start flying into Okinawa, but I didn't know yet if this was actually true.

They should have closed down all the nuclear power

plants the year of the disaster in Fukushima. Why were they so slow to act, when they knew another big earthquake was inevitable? Early in the spring of 2013, when the mass media had started announcing, "The horrors of Fukushima are now over," I spent a week in Kyoto. As a live broadcast from the emperor was scheduled for March 11—the third anniversary of the Fukushima Earthquake—both the hotel staff and all the guests were gathered in the lounge, waiting anxiously for it to begin. Naturally the guest rooms had televisions in them as well, but apparently I wasn't the only one who didn't want to watch this program on their own. Just as a seemingly endless commercial for gargle was beginning to get on my nerves, the screen suddenly went white, then changed to a close-up of a cotton Rising Sun flag blowing in the wind. What came on next was not the face we had been expecting, but a man with a black gauze hood over his face. The entire screen shook. The cameraman must have been trembling. Sticking his neck out toward the microphone like a turtle, the masked man said, "The emperor's wish is that all nuclear plants should be shut down immediately." Everyone in the hotel lounge froze. He went on reassuringly, "There is no need for concern. This is not a kidnapping. I am very closely related to the person who was to have spoken here today," then added, "And we are all in agreement with him." The smooth line from cheek to chin that could be detected through the mask did indeed resemble the face of the emperor doll one sees in displays on Girls' Day.

I hurriedly left the hotel and tried to call my brother, who worked at one of the broadcasting stations, but his cell phone was turned off. Though I tried again several times during the day, I wasn't even able to leave a message. The next day, he finally called to say that he and his family had escaped to their summer cottage in Hyogo Prefecture. As there was a possibility that right-wing terrorists would attack the station on account of the hijacked broadcast, the management had all left Tokyo with their families.

In the end, the station was not attacked. That year, the entire imperial family moved to the palace in Kyoto—as a precaution against the next big earthquake, was the official explanation. It was rumored that they were being held hostage. Unfortunately, there had been no imperial announcements since then.

What happened next was astonishing. The prime minister appeared on the NHK program *Everybody Sing*, and while everyone was wondering what he would perform, he loudly declared, "Next month, all nuclear power plants will be closed down. For good!" This abrupt about-face, coming from someone said to be the most hawkish of hawks, left both hawks and doves with their beaks hanging open. And he stuck to his antinuclear stance as if possessed, despite the efforts of his fellow politicians to make him change his mind: ill-prepared blowfish, home visits from heavily tattooed men, even a laser beam that made the ghost of his father appear in his bedroom to lecture him.

In time, the prime minister disappeared altogether. In more normal circumstances newscasters would have used the word *assassination*, but for some reason they spoke only of "kidnapping." Yet who could have done it? Back when there was still a country called North Korea, the word *kidnapping* was often used, but in 2013, a militant antinuclear movement suddenly emerged in North Korea, providing the impetus for reunification with South Korea.

After a period of unrest following the prime minister's disappearance, in 2015 the Japanese government was privatized; an organization calling itself the Z Group became the major government shareholder and began running the thing as a corporation. Television stations were taken over, and compulsory education was abolished. In Berlin, where I live, I was able for a while to learn about these goings-on in detail from news on the Internet and e-mail from friends, but eventually it became impossible to use the Internet in Japan. Not only could one no longer contact people there in this way, but Japanese websites were not updated. One couldn't call anyone there, either, and letters came back with a post office stamp saying, "No further mail delivery to Japan." In addition, since a German nuclear physicist published a study showing that planes landing in Japan became contaminated by nuclear fallout, there have been no more flights to the country. Although we know about the Great Pacific Earthquake that occurred in 2017, the extent of the damage can only be guessed at from the terrifying images captured by satellite cameras. The tsunami appears to have made a clean sweep from the capital down to the Izu Peninsula. Even now, six years later, the full details are not known. Fortunately, my brother's family had already moved to Hyogo Prefecture. Though I can't contact them directly, my instinct tells me they're all right.

I heard a rumor that you could still fly to Japan from the United States. There was supposed to be a tiny travel company that operated out of the back room of a vegetable shop in Manhattan's Chinatown, where you could buy a ticket to Osaka, but it didn't have a website. Apparently, you had to go there in person, and pay for your ticket in dollars. But after flying all the way to America and following the directions to where the place was supposed to be, I found that the travel agency no longer existed. The people working in the shop told me there actually had been a travel agency operating out of their back room for a while, but one night it suddenly disappeared. Several days of wandering around the area asking people about it failed to turn up even the slightest clue. So, as there was nothing more I could do, I bought some Japanese food that had been flown in from California and went back to Germany. The suitcase I traveled with seems to have disappeared forever.

The summer I went to America, a Portuguese writer who had supposedly sneaked into Japan published a book that was eventually translated into all the European languages, and made quite a splash in the European media. I immediately bought a copy of *The Strange Journey of the Grandson of Fernão Mendes Pinto*, but it was like reading *Gulliver's Travels*. For one thing, since Fernão Mendes Pinto lived in the sixteenth century, the author couldn't possibly be his grandson. Also, in the introduction he said, "As a priest, I went to Japan to save the souls of people who live their lives in the face of death," but according to one newspaper account, he entered the priesthood only immediately before setting off for Japan, having been some sort of adventurer until then. Lying is perhaps a skill that writer-adventurers have to cultivate.

This is the situation as he describes it. All those who were over a hundred years old at the time of the Fukushima nuclear catastrophe in 2011 are still alive; miraculously, not one has died. This is true not only of Fukushima, but of all the twenty-two locations in the central Kanto area that were designated as hot spots in the following years. The oldest woman, who was 120 years of age back then and is much older now, is still very much alive. When Pinto, through an interpreter, complimented her on how well she looked, she replied, "I can't die." It isn't that she has somehow been rejuvenated; it seems, rather, that the radioactive material in the air has robbed her of the ability to die. Unable to sleep at night, she wakes up every morning feeling exhausted, but still has to get up and work. People who were children in 2011, however, are now falling ill one after another, and are not only unable to work, but need constant care. For even if the particles of radiation one is exposed to every day are very small, once they get into your cells and start multiplying, there are soon hundreds of times as many as before. So the younger you are, the greater the damage. But though this was well known in 2011, only a few people immediately fled with their children to southwestern Japan. Several years later, more families finally began to move to places like Okinawa or Hyogo Prefecture. Hyogo made it a policy to favor small businesses that moved in from Tokyo, and there were even some areas where people planning to build houses were given land for free. These new houses were equipped with solar energy, so blackouts were never a problem. The local mountain water was cold and pure, with no radioactive substances detected in it yet. And being close to Kyoto was another benefit: temple delicacies were served as part of the school lunch program; fine ceramics, clothing, and cushions could still be bought. The people who had moved to Hyogo by 2017 were lucky.

For the young, however, "youth" has lost its bloom. Being young now means being too feeble to walk or even stand up, with eyes that can barely see, and mouths that can barely swallow or speak. In the previous century, no one could have predicted that youth could be so painful. What with having to nurse the young and procure food for their families, the old have no energy to spare for anger or grief. In elderly hearts the pain just accumulates, taking no outward form. There are no bodies consumed by flames or rivers of blood, as shown in the hell of Buddhist scrolls with which the situation is now often compared. Patients merely slip from their grasp, however devoted their care, and the youngest die first. And before there's time to think of the future, the next big earthquake comes along. The government assures them that there is no radiation leaking from the four newly destroyed nuclear reactors, but the government is now a private corporation, so no one knows whether or not to believe these announcements.

Pinto came to central Japan during the hottest part of August, when all the doors and windows were left wide open. Words like *robber*, *burglar*, and *thief* were now obsolete. Both men and women wore straw sandals on their bare feet, and commuted to work or school with bare arms and legs. At home, they wore nothing at all. Their nakedness might have made them appear uncivilized to the outside world, their land ripe for colonization, had foreign ships still been coming to Japan. Yet neither black nor white ships appeared in Japanese ports. The sea off Yokohama was dead quiet since no one ate fish or other seafood, or went swimming any longer. Having lost all contact with human beings, the water lay dark and silent. If the gifts from the sea were too dangerous for consumption, so were those from the mountains, like wild mushrooms and other mountain vegetables. In Tokyo they planted string beans and tomatoes in pots filled with cotton instead of earth, which were placed on the roofs of buildings or on verandas.

Pinto reports that there are still some forms of amusement. Every morning people line up in front of rental bookshops and, since there is no electricity to print newspapers, woodblock-printed newssheets are sold in the streets. People perch on the stoops of their houses, playing go or chess. With no television, there is nothing to do during the long evenings but read, yet as the lights go out at sundown, storytellers have appeared to recite the stories of old comic books or animated films to the accompaniment of guitars or lutes. Still, not everyone is satisfied with this weird return to life in the Edo period. Doctors determined to save the lives of victims of radiation gather swarms of fireflies and by this insect light continue after dark to pore over scientific studies and perform experiments, searching for an answer.

Although there are no more computers, pocket games that run on solar batteries are still available. The batteries are so weak, however, that the images move as slowly as actors in a Noh drama. With contests of speed and war games having naturally lost their appeal, something called the Dream Noh Game has cornered the market. The object of this game is to sort out a puzzle of spectral messages from people who died leaving things unsaid or unfulfilled, and to make a story out of them. Players then choose a suitable sutra which, on recitation, will allow the ghost entry to Nirvana. Yet as soon as one ghost disappears, another is there to take its place. The contestant who manages to keep on playing without collapsing out is the winner . . . although hardly anyone remembers what the word *winner* means anymore.

THE CHARM

Kiyoshi Shigematsu

Translated by Jeffrey Hunter

The town that Machiko spent part of her girlhood in was devoured by the ocean.

It was Friday afternoon. Just as she was putting the Girls' Day dolls—which she had lazily left out for a week after the holiday—back into their wooden boxes until it was time to display them again next year, she felt a tremendous shaking, more powerful than any she'd ever experienced.

Later she learned that it had been magnitude 9.0. It was certainly frightening, with the entire apartment building swaying from side to side, but the moment she switched on the television, her concerns about possible damage in Tokyo disappeared.

A map of Japan was on the screen. It showed numbers indicating the quake's magnitude, clustered around the Tohoku area, and moments later, reports on tsunamis appeared. The coastal areas where a "Giant Tsunami Warning" was in effect were outlined in red. The red covered the entire Pacific coastline, from Kanto through Tohoku and up to Hokkaido. The announcer said that some areas were expected to be hit by tsunamis more than three meters high. Of course she had seen "Tsunami Alert" and "Tsunami Warning," but in her nearly fifty years, this was her first "Giant Tsunami Warning."

The predicted height of the tsunami honestly didn't register with her, but her gaze as she watched the TV was drawn to a single point on the map.

The town she'd lived in was in the red zone. She had spent her fourth grade—from April of one year to March of the next—in a town by the seashore, where her father's company had transferred him. The town had a large harbor, filled with fishing boats, and you could hear the cries of seagulls throughout the town, from morning to night.

Please don't let a tsunami hit. These tsunami warnings were usually just a matter of form, really, and later you'd laugh and say, "Well, *that* was a lot of fuss over nothing, wasn't it?" The warning would be called off, the map of Japan would disappear from the TV screen, the program that had been interrupted would pick up where it had left off, and life would go on as usual. She prayed that would be the case again this time.

But the tsunami did hit the town, just as had been warned. Unlike the warning, however, it was not three meters in height. A wall of water over ten meters tall swept over the town, washing several kilometers inland.

The actual event was shown on TV several days later. It had been shot from the roof of the building housing the local fishermen's association. A large fishing boat moored in the harbor had ridden the wave as it swept over the seawall and sped down a street alongside the building. Cars were carried away. The roofs and pillars and walls of homes crushed by the wave were thrown inland with unimaginable force, and then pulled out to sea as the wave withdrew. The video didn't show it, but hundreds of people were also engulfed in the wave.

You could hear the shouts and moans of the young man who was holding the camera. After the wave had swept through the town and was receding in an overpowering vortex to the sea, his moans changed to sobs. Toward the end, perhaps because he was weeping, the camera shook violently. As the lens whipped around, it caught a momentary glimpse of the sky. The heavy gray clouds over the northern town were still the color of winter.

Nearly forty years had passed since Machiko had lived there. Her family had moved around a lot when she was a girl. Each time her father, who worked in the seafood industry, was transferred to a new post, the entire family pulled up stakes and went with him. As a matter of course, each time they moved she transferred to a new school. Nowadays a man on temporary assignment would probably live on his own in an apartment, leaving his family behind and his children in school, but in those days the family stayed together under one roof, no matter what.

Having transferred to so many new schools, she was quite used to saying goodbye to her classmates and, having experienced so many farewells, she easily forgot them.

The same had been true of her friends in this town. While she had continued to exchange New Year's cards with a few of them up through junior high, over time their connection faded naturally, and she had no contact with any of them now. In fact, she couldn't even remember them. So when she heard the report that 754 people were killed or missing, she couldn't picture the face of even a single old school friend.

"I wonder if there's something wrong with me," she said to her husband and children, in a fretful, apologetic tone.

"What do you expect?" her husband said. "It was so long ago. We had a boy who transferred into my fourth-grade class and left after a year, too. I never saw him again, and I certainly don't remember his face, either."

"If it bothers you so much, Mom, why don't you make a donation to the rescue effort or send some relief supplies?"

Picking up on these words of her university-age daughter, her son, who was in his second year at junior high and had just discovered sarcasm, added with a laugh, "Yeah, Mom, send money or some supplies. As a volunteer, you'd just get in the way."

What her husband said was reasonable, her daughter's suggestion was eminently practical, and her son's offhandedness, though it annoyed her as it was intended to, had some truth to it, she had to admit. She understood this, and even accepted it on an intellectual level, but somehow it didn't sit right with her emotionally.

She sent in a donation and mailed packages of relief goods, but the feeling that she hadn't done what was required of her—or what she needed to do—nagged at her. When she thought of the people who had lost their lives, their family members, their homes and belongings, she felt guilty going on with her comfortable, carefree life in Tokyo as if nothing had happened. She felt a need to apologize to someone, to say,

Forgive me. I'm sorry. The fact that she had no idea to whom she could make that apology only made it harder to bear.

Her depression intensified as life in Tokyo began to return to normal—after those first days of staying glued to the TV screen to keep up with the steady flow of reports, then the uproar over the hoarding of mineral water and other supplies, and finally the confusion caused by the rolling blackouts due to the crippled nuclear power plants. In March, her daughter commented that she didn't seem herself, and her son asked her if she was dieting; by April, they were both very worried about her—her daughter suggesting that she might be genuinely ill, and her son commenting on her dramatic weight loss.

Her husband told her that since the earthquake, many were suffering from lethargy and depression. He had read it on an Internet news site. "They identify very strongly with the victims. . . . I feel the same way," he said. "Every morning I examine the list of the dead in the paper, looking for those about our age or who have a family like ours. I think about the dead, and the bitterness and grief of the survivors, and I feel their pain almost like it was my own, while the fact that my life goes on pretty much as it was before the earthquake gives me an indescribable feeling of . . . I don't know . . . shame. People at work ask me to go out drinking like we used to do, but since the disaster it just doesn't feel right going out and having a drink."

"Yes, but maybe that's just what you need, to go out and forget about things," replied Machiko. She made a half-hearted attempt at banter, but she understood how he felt. And for her, there was the additional fact that she had actually lived in a town—though only for one year—that had been devastated by the tsunami. Maybe some of her former classmates were among the dead or missing. It was all the more frustrating and distressing because she had no way of confirming this.

"It's been a terrible shock for everyone, so it's only natural to feel depressed. They say it's better not to dwell on it too much."

"I suppose."

"And, you know, like they say, time heals all wounds. In a few weeks, the TV will go back to its usual mindless variety shows, and we'll forget about the people in the disaster areas. That's how it always goes."

That was true. But somehow, Machiko felt, it mustn't be allowed to be true this time. And at any rate, she was unable to shake off her funk.

"You know, I'm thinking that when things settle down a little bit, I'd like to go there."

"As a volunteer?"

"Not really. I just want to walk around. I want to walk through the town, and if I happen to meet one of my old schoolmates—"

"What would you do?"

Machiko thought about this for a while and just shook her head. "I honestly don't know."

Her husband looked at her with an exasperated expression and sighed. But he didn't tell her not to go.

Machiko got in touch with her mother, who lived in the countryside, and asked her to send photograph albums from when Machiko was a girl.

Unlike today, people weren't constantly snapping photos in those days. There were only about twenty photos from her year there. Most of them were of her family. The only photo of her classmates was one of the entire class soon after she had transferred there.

Perhaps because they all had such stiff, formal expressions, or because it was taken so soon after she had started at a new school, she found it difficult to match the faces with the very faint memories that she retained of her friends there.

She pointed to them one at a time and tried to remember who they were. She couldn't remember the full name of a single one. The first name of one, the last of another, the nickname of a third. Not surprisingly, when she tried comparing these fragmentary memories with the names of evacuation shelter residents listed by the city hall, or the names of the dead and missing from the newspapers, there were no matches.

But it was impossible that none of her thirty-eight classmates had been affected by the disaster. Several must have had their homes washed away, several must have lost loved ones, and perhaps several were themselves no longer of this world.

The clothes and hairstyles of the children in the photograph were unfashionable and unsophisticated. To be honest, they looked shabby, even poor. Machiko stood out. She was quite clearly a city girl.

"Didn't they pick on you because you came from Tokyo?" asked her son.

"No, not at all. They were all very nice to me. They were accepting and kind, and I taught them the games that were popular in Tokyo in those days."

"Games?"

"Well, charms, mostly. Fourth-grade girls like that sort of thing."

"Hmmm."

Her son didn't seem to understand what she was talking about, but her daughter, standing close enough to hear, smiled and nodded.

In fact, Machiko had taught her classmates quite a number of charms.

A charm for getting over nervousness, a charm for avoiding having your teacher call on you when you didn't know the answer, a charm for finding something you'd lost, a charm for making up with a friend . . . Some of the charms Machiko had learned from older girls at her school in Tokyo, and a few she had invented on her own, in response to the needs of her new classmates.

"So you lied to them? That's terrible!"

"It sounds like you deceived them because you thought they were hicks and wouldn't know any better!"

"No, that's just how charms are," said Machiko, overriding her children's protests.

May we meet again, no matter how far away from each other we end up.

It seemed to her she had invented a charm to that effect, too. But she had forgotten the all-important content.

Rearranging her schedule at her part-time job, Machiko was finally able to find the time for a three-day trip just after the weeklong May holiday.

She filled the station wagon with water, food, and whatever relief supplies she could think of, made a reservation at a business hotel outside the town and far enough inland that it was untouched by the disaster, and set out alone from Tokyo.

What was she intending to do? She still had no answer to that question.

She left before dawn and headed north. She got on the expressway and, after passing through the city and suburbs and the scenery changed to open countryside, she realized, very belatedly, that this was the first overnight trip she had taken on her own since she had gotten married twenty-four years ago.

The day was just coming to an end when she arrived at the familiar town—though it had changed so radically that it was no longer familiar to her in the least.

The area near the harbor was a burned-out field. After the tsunami had torn the houses off their foundations, fires broke out and burned for three days and nights. There were many more fishing boats still washed up on land than she had expected. The framing of the refrigerated seafood warehouse had withstood the wave, but the contents had been washed outside by the force of the water. An overpowering stench of rotting fish filled the air as flocks of gulls picked away at the putrefying flesh.

The entire town, however, was not destroyed.

The town was sited at a place where the mountains came down to the sea, so part of it was elevated, inching up the mountain slope. The lower area, close to the water, was known to the locals as the flats, while the area rising up the mountain slope was called the heights.

Machiko had lived in the flats. When she was a girl, that had been the main part of the city, and the heights was little more than terraced vegetable plots, orchards, and a sprinkling of old farmhouses in the traditional style. Kids living in the flats used to ascend the steep roads and paths leading up the mountainside after school with the feeling of going on a field trip or embarking on an adventure; there was also a large, untamed "nature park" in the higher area that offered a wonderful view of the harbor.

But now the heights was very densely developed. The land had been terraced, and rows of houses climbed up the slope. The town hall had been transferred there from the flats several years ago, and in fact the center of town seemed to have moved to this upland section.

While all that remained of the flats was fleets of bulldozers, dump trucks, and Self-Defense Forces vehicles engaged in cleanup and rebuilding, the heights was largely untouched by the earthquake and tsunami. No fires had broken out there, and life went on as it had before the disaster. Boys' Day carp banners were flying in the May breeze.

In that single moment on that single day, the town had been cruelly split apart into two realms—a realm of darkness and a realm of light. Some of the families living in the flats may have been wiped out, while others managed to flee to safety. Though the homes of those in the heights escaped destruction, some families had lost relatives and friends, while others did not. The arbitrariness of it was tragic and bitter.

Machiko drove through the lower part of the town. Not only were all the homes gone, but almost anything that might have enabled her to remember the way it was. She looked at the address signs on the electricity poles, but either the names had been changed or she couldn't place them in the geography of her memory.

Her old school was now an evacuation center. The students had been shifted to a school in the heights, and each classroom was now the temporary home of about ten families. The gymnasium was a distribution center for relief supplies, and its walls had become a giant message board, plastered with notes inquiring about missing family members or giving the temporary addresses where families whose homes had been destroyed were now staying.

Machiko used a corner of the wall.

Before leaving Tokyo, she had scanned her class photo and printed out numerous copies. She clipped them together, hung them on the wall, and added a note of her own.

To the Members of Home Room No. 1, Fourth Grade, 1972, Municipal Elementary School No. 2

Having heard that many people lost all their photo albums in the tsunami, I brought this photo of our class. Please feel free to take a copy.

I am Machiko Harada, a member of the class. My maiden name is Yamamoto. I live in Tokyo now with my husband and two children. I'm seated second from the left in the front row. I transferred into the class from Tokyo in April, at the beginning of the school year, and in the following March, at the end of the school year, my family moved to Sapporo, so I transferred there. My classmates used to call me "Machi." Do you remember me?

When I saw the terrible destruction, I felt I
had to do something, so I've come from Tokyo. If
any of my former classmates reads this note and
remembers who I am, could you please give me a
call at the cell phone number below?

After attaching the letter to the wall, she felt suddenly
anxious. When she had let her children read the letter, they
were scathing:

"I think some people could find it insensitive."

"You haven't suffered anything as a result of the disaster,
but some of those in the evacuation center are certain to have
lost family members, so you really shouldn't write about your
own family in Tokyo."

Her husband defended her, saying, "Let her do it as she
pleases." Then he followed it up with the clincher: "She's not
going to hear from anyone, anyway."

But as a matter of fact, at the time Machiko was confident
her idea would be a success. She was convinced that any of
her former classmates who read the letter would be equally
nostalgic about their past. Now that she had put her note
up on the gymnasium wall, however, that unfounded confi-
dence seemed to reverse itself, transforming into an equally
groundless anxiety.

That night she stayed awake until late in the business
hotel, but her cell phone never rang.

Early the next morning she went back into the town. But
there was nothing for her to do, other than to drive aimlessly
through the piles of debris and rubble. She could sign up as a

volunteer at the town hall, but for a woman approaching fifty with no special skills or training to volunteer for a single day seemed far worse than the bother that her son had chided her for being; it was insensitive to the point of offensiveness.

She drove around town several times. Her cell phone still did not ring.

As she neared the harbor, there were many puddles in the streets. She encountered a woman and her children cleaning up the rubble of their home and scraping away the mud with a shovel. Just like Machiko's own family, there was an older daughter and a younger son. They were about the same age as her own children, in fact. Maybe the father wasn't there because he was at work. Or maybe . . .

She drove past the house and stopped the car. Perhaps there was something she could do to help. But when she had turned off the engine and undone her seat belt, she suddenly felt a great heaviness in her heart. She sighed. After murmuring, "More a bother than a help," she no longer felt the energy to get out of the car.

She had no idea whether they would actually take offense; she just decided on her own that they would. In fact, though she might not have been much practical help, the mother and her children may have been glad just to have someone offer.

But no—no, they wouldn't. Something was wrong about it. Something was deeply inappropriate. She started the engine again and drove off. She accelerated rapidly on the dusty road, its blacktop paving torn off by the tsunami. She was glad she hadn't gotten out of the car. She should have realized earlier that there are some times when a woman shouldn't meddle, even with the best of intentions.

She passed the boundary of downtown and got onto the

highway. Heading for a city farther inland, that hadn't been harmed by the tsunami, she accelerated again. She seemed to be turning her back on this town of her girlhood, to be fleeing.

What am I doing?

She had no idea.

You're too old for this nonsense.

No, it was precisely because of her age that she was floundering so gracelessly.

The cell phone had still not rung.

Rather than feeling bad about it, she found herself relieved.

She drove for a long, long time, until evening. She drove around and around her old town, in circles.

Whenever she saw a convenience store, she would stop, get out of the car, and put money in the collection box for contributions to help those afflicted by the disaster that was invariably sitting next to the register. Her contributions were like excuses, she thought, like apologies.

To whom? For what?

Here she was, and it was no different from when she lay wallowing in depression back in Tokyo.

She drove back to the town at evening, as if to say goodbye. She went to the old "nature park" on the mountainside, to bring her trip to a close by looking out over the town.

When she was a girl, it was an almost untouched wild space, bordered on three sides by woods. The woods had now been completely replaced with houses, and the sign over the entrance read "Children's Park."

The excellence of the view of the town and the ocean,

however, remained unchanged. The swings faced the sea. She remembered swinging on them, soaring higher and higher until a giddy, uncontrollable thrill rose in her chest and she felt as if her momentum would send her flying through the bottomless, open sky before her. Seeing that the swings were still in the same place, she thought that today's elementary school students must gulp with that same giddy thrill, when suddenly she experienced a flash of recall.

"Yes, yes!" she almost said aloud.

A forgotten memory suddenly came back to her. For the first time since returning here, she remembered, clearly, the face of one of her friends.

She was playing in the park with Keiko, her best friend, soon after she had learned that at the end of the school year she would be moving and transferring to a new school.

Graduation was approaching quickly; not many days were left before they'd have to say goodbye. Keiko was very sad that Machiko was leaving, and she asked her to teach her a charm that would enable her to be reunited with a friend who had moved away.

Machiko didn't know a charm for that. But to please Keiko, and because she fervently wanted to believe in such a charm herself, she invented one on the spur of the moment:

There were two swings in the park. They had to sit on the swings and push off, timing their arcs so that as one swung forward, the other swung backward, higher and higher. After they had each swung thirty times, the charm started. When your swing flew forward, you called out the other's name. You repeated this ten times. Then you swung in this alter-

nating rhythm ten more times, calling out when you wanted
to meet. Throughout all of this, you could not look at your
friend's face. You were to look straight ahead and say when
you would meet—as quickly as you could, before the swing
went backward again.

It was a fine charm, Machiko thought, even if she had just
come up with it on the spot. The parts about not looking at
your friend and speaking as quickly as possible were exactly
the special touches you looked for in a charm.

"Everyone in Tokyo is doing it"—that little white lie was
the perfect finishing touch. Keiko accepted it unquestion-
ingly, and she immediately said, "Let's do it. Let's do it now!"
and they climbed on the swings.

Keiko was very trusting, thought Machiko with a wry
smile as she sat there on the bench and took the class photo
out of her purse. There she was: second row, fourth from the
right. Diagonally behind their homeroom teacher. *She's this
one, with the face of a country girl;* as Machiko lightly brought
her finger to the face of the girl with the bangs and straight
shoulder-length hair, she felt a tiny bit better.

What was the day they had set for their reunion? She
didn't remember. Probably something like "summer vacation." Or, unable to wait for summer, had they set it for the
Golden Week string of holidays in May? Whatever it had
been, the charm had not worked. Machiko moved away the
day after graduation and never saw Keiko again.

*I wonder how Keiko is? I hope she got married, left this town, and
is living happily with her family in a place far from the destruction here.*
Not just Keiko. *Everyone. Everyone. Everyone. Everyone.* Looking
at her class photo, her eyes and fingers going over each of her
classmates, she prayed with all her heart that everyone had
survived.

But praying isn't enough. I'm going to swing. I'm going to believe the charm. Maybe this time it will work.

She rose from the bench and walked toward the swings.

Just then two elementary school girls came into the park. Their book bags strapped to their backs, they were probably stopping to play on the way home.

"We're in luck! They're free!" cried one happily.

"Let's hurry!" shouted the other, and they ran hand in hand to the swings.

I wonder what grade they're in, thought Machiko. They look like fourth or fifth graders. They seemed a little old for swings, but maybe it was because they were country girls, more innocent than girls their age in Tokyo. She smiled at the thought. She sat back down on the bench, relinquishing the swings to them.

The girls both immediately stood up on the seats, looked at each other as if coordinating some kind of prearranged plan, and began swinging.

Forward, back, forward, back, forward, back . . . The two swings were moving forward in an alternating rhythm. "One, two, three . . ." Each girl counted her swings as she went forward. When they reached thirty, they began shouting out each other's name.

"Eri-chan!"

"Haruka-chan!"

"Eri-chan!"

"Haruka-chan!"

"Eri-chan!"

"Haruka-chan!"

"Eri-chan!"

"Haruka-chan!"

The girls called the names out quickly, ten times each.

Then they each took turns shouting, again as quickly as they could, the same phrase, alternating as each swung forward, ten times:

"Summer vacation!"

"Summer vacation!"

"Summer vacation!"

"Summer vacation!"

Machiko rose from the bench and stared at the girls in astonishment.

They were both fourth-grade students at Municipal Elementary School No. 2. They were best friends. All the members of both their families were safe, but their homes, in the flats, had been carried away by the tsunami and their neighborhoods burned in the fires that followed. They were presently living in an evacuation center and attending school in the heights, but one of them would soon be moving away with her family to stay with relatives outside the town. They would be separated.

But they wanted to see each other again.

They wanted to play together again.

When Machiko asked about the charm they had just made, the girl who was leaving said that a sixth grader had taught it to her, and the girl who was staying behind added proudly that it was a tradition that had been passed down for many, many years at Municipal Elementary School No. 2.

"Yes, a tradition. My father went to Municipal Elementary School No. 2, and he said they had that charm from his time there. No other school knows it; it's just ours."

"The sixth grader said that it's very powerful."

"It can make miracles happen."

"So I know I'll see Eri-chan again."

"Yes, for sure. We'll see each other again."

Keiko had taught it to one of her friends. *Yes, that must be it.* And then that friend had taught it to another, and it had spread to younger students, eventually becoming a school tradition, being passed on from generation to generation. . . .

"Hey, lady, are you crying?"

"Why? Did I say something wrong?"

"She's really crying."

"I'm sorry! Why?"

Machiko understood. The one she had wanted to meet most of all in the town was herself—herself from long ago. And now everything was all right. *She was still there.* Here was the proof that she had lived here.

The heavy feeling in her chest quietly evaporated. At last she felt that she could weep for someone. "You don't have to suffer under that pall of depression, unable to remember any-one's face"—someone in her mind, someone whose face she couldn't see, seemed to be speaking to her and softly patting her back.

After the two girls had left the park and the tracks of her tears had dried, her cell phone rang.

It must be Keiko—but the moment she thought that, she knew it was too neat.

It was a man. It was one of the boys in her class. He said his name was Hasegawa. He had just seen the photograph in the gymnasium. It filled him with nostalgia, and it made him very happy, he said.

Hasegawa . . . Hasegawa . . . Hasegawa . . . With the photograph in hand, Machiko searched her memory, but to no avail. He spoke to her with a degree of formality that seemed to indicate that he didn't actually remember her, either.

Maybe if she asked him to tell her where he was in the photo, she'd remember him.

Machiko lifted her gaze from the photograph and looked toward the devastated plain of the town. She focused on it. She felt tears rising in her eyes again.

"You came all the way from Tokyo because of the photograph?"

"Yes, well . . ."

"And where are you now?"

After blinking forcefully and shaking the tears from her eyes, Machiko said, "I'm sorry. I'm already back in Tokyo."

"Oh, I see. I'm sorry I didn't notice your message earlier, since you'd traveled all that way."

"I'll come again," she replied with a decisiveness that surprised her. And pleased her.

Hasegawa seemed equally pleased by her reply. "Yes, certainly. Please come again," he said in a voice suddenly garbled with emotion.

"We're all having a hard time right now, and my family has been living in an evacuation center since the quake. My mother is still missing. . . . But please come again next spring. . . . Or if you can't make it, then the year after or the year after that, when everyone is back on their feet and the town is rebuilt. We'll have a reunion."

Yes, she replied. But it wasn't enough. As she said it, she bowed deeply in the direction of the town she loved and remembered.

She ended the call and stood on the seat of one of the swings.

How many years had it been since she'd been on a swing? She hadn't been to a park since her son had gone off to elementary school, so it must be nearly a decade. And considerably more since she had stood up on a swing seat—maybe two decades.

The seat was much less stable than she had anticipated, and the chains shook as she twisted them. But the swing moved slowly. At first the arc was small, but slowly she gained momentum.

Her charm would start with "Everyone" ten times.

Then "Next spring" ten times.

She bent her knees, then straightened them again, using the recoil to power the swing.

In front of her, the town she remembered so fondly began to sway.

NIGHTCAP

Yoko Ogawa

Translated by Stephen Snyder

When the world brings you anxiety and pain, nothing is as devastating as a sleepless night. You know perfectly well that worrying will do no good, but you worry still, shed tears all night long. And when dawn approaches, there's no solution, just a feeling of utter hopelessness—and the tears, so many you wonder how your body could have cried them all. I prefer to avoid such nights if possible, to sleep instead. A person may be poor and ignorant, may be afflicted with illness and suffering, but if he can sleep at night, he'll survive.

The nightcap is made of wool, hand-knitted of thick yarn. The stitch is loose, the color dark. On top, there's a pom-pom the size of a Ping-Pong ball, and somehow only there can the mottled pattern of the yarn be seen. The pom-pom is so appealing, so touchable that it bears traces of the

many hands that have rubbed it. If you don this cap at bed-
time, you will sleep through the night free of worry and
tears.

Everyone needs one—there are even versions for pets.
Dogs, cats, sparrows, turtles, rabbits, goats, giant flying squirrels, armadillos, walruses—a nightcap for each, and with it
the peace of sleep. What's more, the nightcap is ideal in an
emergency; when disaster strikes and you have to flee, it can
be folded up and stuffed in your pocket—like Snufkin setting out from Moomin Valley with nothing but his harmon-
ica. After all, no matter where you go, no matter where you
find yourself, you need to sleep, to rest. Even when all is lost,
when there is no refuge in the waking world, the nightcap and
sleep remain. You can still find repose in the land of sleep,
gently rubbing the pom-pom, free of all worry.

GOD BLESS YOU, 2011

Hiromi Kawakami

Translated by Ted Goossen and Motoyuki Shibata

The bear invited me to go for a walk to the river, about twenty minutes away. I had taken that road once before in the early spring to see the snipes, but then I had worn protective clothing; now it was hot, and for the first time since the "incident" I would be clad in normal clothes that exposed the skin, and carrying a box lunch to boot. It would be a bit of a trek, somewhere between a hike and a stroll.

The bear was a massive full-grown male who had just moved into apartment 305, three doors down the hall from me. As a gesture of goodwill, he had presented the three of us who remained in the building with "moving-in noodles" and packets of postcards, a level of formality you don't see often nowadays. *He sure wants people to like him,* I thought, but then you probably have to do that if you're a bear.

When he stopped by my apartment with the noodles, we discovered that we might not be complete strangers after all.

"You don't happen to be from X town, do you?" he asked when he saw my name on the door. Yes, I replied, I certainly am. It turned out that a person who had been a huge help to him when he was in the evacuation center there during the "incident" had an uncle, one of the town officials, whose last name matched mine. When we traced the connection a bit further, we arrived at the conclusion that this official and my father might be second cousins. A flimsy tie, to be sure, but the bear appeared deeply moved nonetheless, waxing eloquently about the "karmic bond" it established between us. From his moving-in etiquette to his manner of speech, he seemed to be an old-fashioned type of bear indeed.

And so the bear and I headed down the road on our stroll, which might better have been termed a hike. I don't know a whole lot about the animal kingdom, so I couldn't tell if he was an Asiatic black bear, a brown bear, or a Malayan sun bear. I thought of asking him, but it seemed rude. Nor did I know his name. When I asked what I should call him, he thought for a moment and then, after checking to be sure no other bears were nearby, said: "For the moment I am without a name, and since there are no other bears here, I don't think I really need one. I prefer to be addressed as 'you,' but please imagine it written in Chinese characters, not phonetically. Actually, though, you can call me anything you like—I won't mind."

Yes, this was a most old-fashioned bear. Not to mention rather finicky about trivial points of logic.

The road to the river ran through a strip of land that had once been rice paddies. Almost all the paddies had been turned up during the process of decontamination, however, and now the earth lay in glistening piles. Despite the heat, all the workers we saw were wearing cumbersome protective suits, masks, and waders that extended up to their waists. For several years after the "incident," entry to this area had been absolutely forbidden and the deep cracks in the road left untouched, but recently the whole road had been repaved. Although Ground Zero was close by, a surprising number of cars passed us. They slowed to a crawl as they approached and made a wide circle around us. Not a soul passed on foot.

"Maybe they're keeping a distance because we're not wearing protective suits," I said. The bear grunted. "I took special care to avoid too much radiation the first half of this year, so my total amount of accumulated radiation indicates I can still afford some exposure. And SPEEDI (the System for Prediction of Environmental Dose Information) predicts we won't have a lot of wind in this region."

The bear responded to my apparent excuses with a vague shrug. The only sound was the rhythmic crunch of his paws on the pavement.

I asked if he was hot.

"No, I'm fine. Walking on asphalt is a bit tiring, but I'll be okay. The river's not that far. Thank you for your concern. It's kind of you to . . . Of course if *you* are hot we can walk on the shoulder. My body is much larger than yours, so my maximum permissible dose is much higher, which means it should be all right for me to go without shoes where the radiation levels are worse. It'll be cooler for you than this hot pavement. Shall we move?"

He went on in this vein, a model of solicitude. I was wearing a big hat and can handle heat well anyway, so I said no, but in fact it may have been he who wanted to move off the pavement. We walked on silently.

Eventually we heard in the distance the faint sound of rushing water. As we walked it grew louder until, at last, we reached the river. I had expected to find no one there, but two men were standing by the water's edge. Before the "incident," this had been a lively place where people swam and fished, and families brought their children. Now, however, there were no children left anywhere in the area.

I set down my bag and started mopping my face with a towel. The bear's tongue was hanging out, and he was panting slightly. As we stood there, the two men came up to us. Both were wearing protective suits. One had long gloves that reached his elbows, while the other sported sunglasses.

"It's a bear, isn't it," said Sunglasses.

"I envy bears," replied Long Gloves.

"Bears can handle strontium. Plutonium, too."

"What do you expect? They're bears."

"So that's why. Because they're bears."

"Yeah, because they're bears."

They went back and forth like this a few more times. Sunglasses stole a glance at my face, but he avoided looking at the bear directly. Long Gloves occasionally ran his hands over the bear's belly and tugged at his fur. Finally they said, "Because he's a bear," one last time, turned their backs, and wandered off.

"Good grief," the bear said after they had gone. "I guess they meant well."

I didn't say anything.

"You know, my maximum permissible dose may be a bit higher than for humans, but that doesn't mean I'm resistant to strontium and plutonium. Oh well, how can you expect them to know?"

Before I had a chance to reply, the bear walked quickly to the river's edge.

A small fish was darting back and forth. The cool of the river felt good on my face. Looking more closely, I could see that the fish was swimming in a narrowly circumscribed area, first upstream, then downstream, as if bound by a long and narrow rectangular space. Those bounds marked its turf. The bear was studying the water also. But was he seeing the same things that I was? Perhaps the world beneath the water was different when seen through the eyes of a bear.

Suddenly, there was a great splash as the bear leaped into the river. When he had sloshed halfway across he stopped, plunged his right paw into the current, and pulled out a fish. It was about three times the size of the small fish we had seen swimming along the banks.

"Bet you were surprised," the bear said when he had returned. "My legs just moved on their own. Good-sized one, isn't it?"

The bear held the fish up for me to see. Its fins sparkled in the sunlight. The two men from before were pointing in our direction and saying something to each other. The bear beamed triumphantly.

"They eat the moss that grows on the river bottom," he said. "Unfortunately, a lot of cesium collects there, too."

The bear opened his bag, pulled out a cloth bundle, and withdrew a small knife and a cutting board. Deftly he cut open the fish, gutted it, and washed it with water from a plastic bottle he had brought for the occasion. Then he sprinkled it liberally with coarse salt and laid it on a large leaf.

"If we turn it over every so often it'll be ready to eat by the time we get back home," he said. "But even if you don't eat it, it'll be a nice reminder of our trip together."

This bear really thinks of everything, I thought admiringly.

We spread a cloth on a bench and sat there looking at the river and eating the lunches we had packed. The bear had notched a stick of French bread and inserted pâté and radishes into the openings, while I had rice balls with pickled plum in the middle. For dessert we had one orange each. It was a leisurely meal.

"Might I have your orange peel?" he said after we had finished. I gave it to him, and he turned his back to me and gobbled it down.

The bear went to flip the fish over, then carefully washed the knife, cutting board, and cups with water from the bottle. After drying them, he extracted a large towel from his bag and handed it to me.

"Please use this when you take your nap. It has only been two hours since we started out, and the radioactivity is low, but all the same . . . I'm off to take a little walk. Would you like me to sing you a lullaby before I go?" he asked earnestly.

I told him I was quite capable of falling asleep without a lullaby. He was clearly disappointed, but a moment later he was headed upstream on his walk.

When I awoke, the shadows of the trees had lengthened and the bear was sleeping on the bench beside mine. No towel was covering his body, and he was snoring faintly. Apart from us, the place was deserted. The two men were nowhere to be seen. I laid the towel on the bear and went to turn over the salted fish. There were three fish now where only one had been before.

"What a fine outing!" the bear said, standing before apartment 305. He pulled a Geiger counter out of his bag and ran it over first my body, then his own. I heard the familiar beeping. "I hope we have occasion to do it again."

I nodded. When I thanked him for the salted fish and everything else, he waved it off.

"Not at all," he answered.

"Okay then . . ." I said, turning to leave.

"Well . . ." He hesitated shyly.

I waited for him to go on, but he just stood there fidgeting. He was a truly massive bear. A gurgling sound came from deep in his throat. When he was talking, his voice sounded entirely human, but when he hemmed and hawed like this, or when he laughed, he sounded like a real bear.

"Would you mind if we hugged?" he finally asked. "Where I come from, that's what we do when we say good-bye to someone we feel close to. If you don't like the idea, of course, then we don't have to."

I consented. The fact that bears don't take baths meant there would probably be more radiation on his body. But it had been my decision from the start to remain in this part of the country, so I could hardly be squeamish.

The bear took a step forward, spread his arms wide, and embraced my shoulders. Then he pressed his cheek against mine. I could smell the odor of bear. He moved his other cheek to mine and squeezed me firmly again. His body was cooler than I had expected.

"I had a truly wonderful time. I feel as though I have returned from a voyage to some faraway place. May the bear god bestow his blessings on you. Oh yes, salted fish doesn't keep very well, so if you choose not to eat it be sure to throw it out tomorrow."

Back in my apartment, I placed the wrapped salted fish atop the shoe cabinet in the entrance and went in to take a shower. I carefully washed my hair and body, then sat down to write in my diary before going to bed. As I do every night, I recorded my estimate of the radiation I had received that day: 30 microsieverts on the surface of my body, and 19 microsieverts of internally received radiation. For the year to date, 2,900 microsieverts of external radiation, and 1,780 microsieverts of internal radiation. I tried picturing what the bear god looked like, but it was beyond my imagination. All in all, it had been a pretty good day.

POSTSCRIPT

I wrote "Kami-sama," translated here as "God Bless You," in 1993.

The title in Japanese literally means "God," and I make reference to a bear god in the story.

Many such gods existed in ancient Japan. There were gods who presided over all aspects of greater nature: gods of the mountains, of the ocean and the rivers, of the wind and the rain. There were gods connected to daily life as well: gods of the rice fields, of human habitations, of the hearth, the toilet, and the well. Gods who punished, animal gods. There were demons, too, and giants, goblins, and tree spirits that ranged across Japan, from the north of the archipelago all the way down to Okinawa.

It would be an exaggeration to say that I believe in all these gods from the depths of my heart; yet when I awake on a heaterless morning in these days of electricity rationing and feel the warm rays of the sun pouring through my window, my immediate reaction is "Aah, the sun god has returned." In that sense, I still retain the sensibility of the Japanese of old.

My reaction to all that I saw and heard in the aftermath of the earthquake was "Why have I kept myself in the dark all these years, never attempting to find out what I should have known?" What follows, therefore, is an account of the few things I have learned since then. Since I am not an expert, my terms and metaphors may sometimes be off the mark. If so, I hope those of you reading this will help me correct my mistakes.

First, uranium.

The radioactive isotopes used to power nuclear plants like those in Fukushima are obtained from a material called uranium-235. These isotopes are found in nature, in the uranium that is buried in mountains, or deep in the earth, or even directly under towns and cities.

Natural uranium, however, contains two types of radioactive isotopes, which are known as uranium-235 and uranium-238. U-238 is far more common than U-235.

Indeed, put in more familiar terms, uranium-238 comprises 99.3 percent of all natural uranium; uranium-235 just 0.7 percent.

In other words, uranium-235 is extremely rare.

Human beings have managed to condense this rare mineral to generate electrical power, or build bombs like the one dropped on Hiroshima. When U-238 is bombarded with those light and airy particles called neutrons it remains aloof and unconcerned, while the same neutrons set off a rapid chain reaction in the more unstable U-235. The point being, I guess, that a guy who is quick to fly off the handle generates more energy than a guy who is mellow and easygoing.

When I watch the daily reports of the explosive incidents at the nuclear plant and the "critical" situation there, I wonder how the god of uranium feels about the fact that we have set the gremlins of U-235 to work for us in this fashion.

As I said, uranium-235 is exceedingly rare. As a matter of fact, though, it was more common back in the old days. The old days here being about 4.5 billion years ago. A time not long after the earth was formed.

The life of U-235, however, is shorter than that of U-238; indeed, the half-life of U-238 is 4.5 billion years, while it takes only 740 million years for half of U-235 to give up the ghost. So over all these billions of years, the population of U-235 was dwindling away there unnoticed in the ground, shrinking by half every 740 million years. And then humans came across it.

It was Marie and Pierre Curie who discovered the presence of radioactive isotopes in the late nineteenth century. Then, eventually, World War II came along. Well, people thought, let's put these guys to work for us now. And they didn't fool around, either. Germany concentrated more on nuclear power, while countries like the United States, Great Britain, Russia, and Japan focused on nuclear bombs.

But let me return to the story of the god of uranium.

Uranium-235 had been resting there in the ground, quietly dwindling away for billions of years. Had no human touched it, it would have gone on peacefully emitting its piddling quantities of radiation without causing any problem. "How self-effacing we are!" I can hear the god say. "Per time-and-space unit, our radiation is far less than that of the cosmic rays that bombard the earth every day."

Human beings, however, had another idea. They gathered bits of U-235 from wherever they lay, concentrated them, and then whipped them into action. "Split your atoms," they cried. "Give us light, give us heat, give us power. Work! Work!" For nuclear bombs, they demanded that the power be released in great explosions; for nuclear power, in dribs and drabs . . .

If the god of uranium really exists, then what must he be thinking? Were this a fairy tale of old, what would happen when humans break the laws of nature and turn gods into minions?

In 2011, I reworked "God Bless You," below, into "God Bless You, 2011." I had no intention of standing in the pulpit and preaching against the dangers of nuclear power. Rather, my purpose was to express my amazement at how our daily lives can go on uneventfully day after day and then suddenly be so dramatically changed by external events. The experience left me with a quiet anger that still has not subsided. Yet, in the end, this anger is directed at nothing other than myself. Who built today's Japan if not me—and others like me? Even as we bear this anger, we carry on in our mundane lives. Stubbornly, we refuse to give up, to say the hell with it. For when all is said and done, it is always a joy to be alive, however daunting the circumstances may be.

GOD BLESS YOU
✳ THE ORIGINAL 1993 VERSION ✳

The bear invited me to go for a walk to the river, about twenty minutes away. I had taken that road once before in the early spring to see the snipes, but this was the first time I had gone in hot weather, and carrying a box lunch to boot. It would be a bit of a trek, somewhere between a hike and a stroll.

The bear was a massive full-grown male who had just moved into apartment 305, three doors down the hall from me. As a gesture of goodwill, he had presented all of us on the same floor with "moving-in noodles" and packets of postcards, a level of formality you don't see often nowadays. *He sure wants people to like him,* I thought, but then you probably have to do that if you're a bear.

When he stopped by my apartment with the noodles, we discovered that we might not be complete strangers after all.

"You don't happen to be from X town, do you?" he asked when he saw my name on the door. Yes, I replied, I certainly am. It turned out that a person who had once been a huge help to him had an uncle, one of the town officials, whose last name matched mine. When we traced the connection a bit further, we arrived at the conclusion that this official and my father might be second cousins. A flimsy tie, to be sure, but the bear appeared deeply moved nonetheless, waxing eloquently about the "karmic bond" it established between us. From his moving-in etiquette to his manner of speech, he seemed to be an old-fashioned type of bear indeed.

✳

And so the bear and I headed down the road on our stroll,
which might better have been called a hike. I don't know a
whole lot about the animal kingdom, so I couldn't tell if he
was an Asiatic black bear, a brown bear, or a Malayan sun
bear. I thought of asking him, but it seemed too rude. Nor
did I know his name. When I asked what I should call him,
he thought for a moment and then, after checking to be sure
no other bears were nearby, said: "For the moment I am without a name, and since there are no other bears here, I don't
think I really need one. I prefer to be addressed as 'you,' but
please imagine it written in Chinese characters, not phonetically. Actually, though, you can call me anything you like—I
won't mind."

Yes, this was a most old-fashioned bear. Not to mention
rather finicky about trivial points of logic.

The road to the river ran though rice paddies. It was a paved
road, and cars drove past from time to time. They slowed to
a crawl as they approached and made a wide circle around us.
Not a soul passed on foot. It was a scorching day, and no one
was working in the paddies. The only sound was the rhythmic crunch of the bear's paws on the pavement.

I asked if he was hot.

"No, I'm fine. Walking on asphalt is a bit tiring, but I'll
be okay. The river's not that far. Thank you for your concern.
It's kind of you to . . . Of course if *you* are hot we can find a
place to rest on the main highway."

He continued in this vein, a model of solicitude. I was
wearing a big hat and can handle heat well anyway, so I said

no, but in fact it may have been he who wanted to take a
break. We walked on silently.

Eventually we heard in the distance the faint sound of
rushing water. As we walked it grew louder until, at last, we
reached the river. Many people were gathered on its banks,
some swimming, others fishing. I set down my bag and
started mopping my face with a towel. The bear's tongue was
hanging out, and he was panting slightly. As we stood there
two men and a young boy came up to us. All three were wearing swimming trunks. One man sported sunglasses while the
other had a snorkel draped around his neck.

"Daddy, it's a bear!" squealed the boy.

"Right you are," said Snorkel.

"A real bear!"

"A bear for sure."

"A bear! A bear!"

They went back and forth like this a few more times.
Snorkel stole a glance at my face, but he avoided looking at the
bear directly. Sunglasses just stood there silently. The child
yanked the bear's fur and kicked his legs. Then he shouted,
"Punch!" and slugged the bear in the stomach before running off. The two men ambled after him.

"Good grief," the bear said after they had gone. "But
young people don't mean any harm, you know."

I didn't say anything.

"I mean, human beings are of all sorts, but children have
no real malice."

Before I had a chance to reply, the bear walked quickly to
the river's edge.

A small fish was darting back and forth. The cool of the
river felt good on my face. Looking more closely, I could see

that the fish was swimming in a narrowly circumscribed area, first upstream, then downstream, as if bound by a long and narrow rectangular space. Those bounds marked its turf. The bear was studying the water also. But was he seeing the same things that I was? Perhaps the world beneath the water was different when seen through the eyes of a bear.

Suddenly, there was a great splash as the bear leaped into the river. When he had sloshed halfway across he stopped, plunged his right paw into the current, and pulled out a fish. It was about three times the size of the fish we had seen swimming along the banks.

"Bet you were surprised," the bear said when he had returned. "I should have warned you, but my legs moved on their own. Good-sized one, isn't it?"

The bear held the fish up for me to see. Its fins sparkled in the sunlight. People fishing along the shore were pointing in our direction and saying something to each other. The bear beamed triumphantly.

"Allow me to give you this fish. As a memento of our day together."

The bear opened his bag, pulled out a cloth bundle, and withdrew a small knife and a cutting board. Deftly he cut open the fish, gutted it, and washed it. Then he sprinkled it liberally with coarse salt he had brought for the occasion and laid it on a large leaf.

"If we turn it over every so often it'll be ready to eat by the time we get back home," he said.

This bear really thinks of everything, I thought admiringly.

We sat there on the grass looking at the river and eating the lunches we had packed. The bear had notched a stick of French bread and inserted pâté and radishes into the openings; while I had rice balls with pickled ume in the middle. For dessert we had one orange each. It was a leisurely meal.

"Might I have your orange peel?" he said after we had finished. I gave it to him, and he turned his back to me and gobbled it down.

The bear went to flip the fish over, then carefully washed the knife, cutting board, and cups with water from the river. After drying them, he extracted a large towel from his bag and handed it to me.

"Please use this when you take your nap. I'm off to take a little walk. Would you like me to sing you a lullaby before I go?" he asked earnestly.

I told him I was quite capable of falling asleep without a lullaby. He was clearly disappointed, but a moment later he was headed upstream on his walk.

When I awoke the shadows of the trees had lengthened and the bear was sleeping beside me on the ground. No towel was covering his body, and he was snoring faintly. Only a few people remained along the bank. All of them were fishing. I laid the towel on the bear and went to turn over the salted fish. There were three fish now where only one had been before.

"What a fine outing!" the bear said, standing before apartment 305 and pulling his keys from his bag. "I hope we have occasion to do it again."

I nodded. When I thanked him for the salted fish and everything else, he waved it off.

"Not at all," he answered.

"Okay then . . ." I said, turning to leave.

"Well . . ." He hesitated shyly.

I waited for him to go on, but he just stood there fidgeting. He was a truly massive bear. A gurgling sound came from deep in his throat. When he was talking, his voice sounded entirely human, but when he hemmed and hawed like this, or when he laughed, he sounded like a real bear.

"Would you mind if we hugged?" he finally asked. "Where I come from, that's what we do when we say good-bye to someone we feel close to. If you don't like the idea, of course, then we don't have to."

I consented. The bear took a step forward, spread his arms wide, and embraced my shoulders. Then he pressed his cheek against mine. I could smell the odor of bear. He moved his other cheek to mine and squeezed me firmly again. His body was cooler than I had expected.

"I had a truly wonderful time. I feel as though I have returned from a voyage to some faraway place. May the bear god bestow his blessings on you. Oh yes, and salted fish doesn't keep very well, so make sure you eat it all this evening."

Back in my apartment, I grilled the salted fish and took a bath. Then I wrote a bit in my diary before going to bed. I tried picturing what the bear god looked like, but it was beyond my imagination. All in all, it had been a pretty good day.

MARCH YARN

Mieko Kawakami

Translated by Michael Emmerich

I'm so not looking forward to tomorrow, everything going back to normal," she said as she thumped her calves with her fists, her tone genuinely despondent. "It's always the same thing, again and again, and before you know it, your life is over. The fun things happen so quickly, and the rest, the stuff that wears you down, it just keeps coming. You get these little slivers of life to fill in whatever time is left, and that's it." She sighed. The sound of her fists slapping her calves grew louder. "Look at this swelling. They don't even look like my legs."

A little past one in the afternoon, we arrived in Kyoto.

We were on our way home after visiting her parents in Shimane. She had decided not to stay with them for the birth, so we figured we'd better go to see them while we were still mobile. Then, out of nowhere, she suggested that since we wouldn't be able to travel for a while once the baby was born, we should go somewhere on the way home. We had never traveled much, and the thought of randomly choosing a destination, booking a hotel, and staying there with no clear purpose was just added stress. But I told her it was fine, not saying anything more. After a while she sighed. "If you don't want to do it, just say so." The truth was, it was draining enough getting ready to make the thousand-plus-kilometer trip back home with a wife eight months pregnant and I wasn't eager to add a bit of unanticipated sightseeing, but I kept that to myself. She shot me a glance and then, making a face like what's the problem?, she punched away at her cell phone, did a few searches for tourist spots and hotels, and said, "How about Kyoto? This is just the season for a trip to Kyoto."

It was too early to check in to our hotel in the vast expanse of Kyoto Station, so we decided to leave our luggage at the front desk and go to Kiyomizu Temple.

We weren't especially excited about seeing the temple, but the concierge recommended it as the "liveliest" tourist spot. We checked the destinations for the buses that kept rolling into the rotary, and after about ten minutes we got on one. Even though it was a weekday, both the plaza in front of the station and the bus itself were packed with tourists and young couples. Fortunately a large white woman noticed my wife's belly and let her have her seat. The woman's smile made me think of some sort of fruit split down the middle.

*

"Oh no, this is much too steep," she said. "There's no way."

The bus made its way through traffic, and in about ten minutes we got to our stop. We walked quite a while, following the crowd, until we came to the wide flight of steps that led to the temple. Then she looked up and decided she'd rather not.

"You aren't feeling well?"

"It's not that. But just look, there's no way I can climb these steps. Let's just get tea somewhere and go back to the hotel."

We settled on a random café among the crowd of souvenir shops.

As we were waiting for our drinks, I folded my arms and closed my eyes.

"Why are you so sleepy all the time?" she grumbled. "You sleep just fine."

I would have liked to say that you don't need a reason to be sleepy, but whenever I see that look in her eyes, like she's waiting for me to say something, the words die on my lips.

"I don't know," I said. "Maybe I don't sleep deeply enough."

"You're always like this now. You didn't used to be. Why are you so tired?"

"I really don't know. Something about the way I'm sleeping, I guess."

"Yeah," she said, "just wait until the baby is born. You know how many times we'll have to get up every night, right? We're in paradise now, compared with that."

"I know."

My iced coffee and her iced tea with lemon came; we drank in silence.

"The thing I want to know," she said eventually, "is why the tiresome things in life always overwhelm the fun stuff. That's the question."

She talked as if she were picking up the thread of an earlier conversation, but she wasn't and I didn't know what she was talking about. I just mumbled something and stared blankly at the needles of light radiating from her glass.

"Why are fun things always followed by something dreary?"

"You don't like having them alternate, is that it?"

"That's not what I'm saying. After you have fun, something dreary happens afterward, right? Every single time, without fail. That's what bothers me."

"The order, you mean?"

"No, the amount."

I didn't understand what she was getting at or what I was saying in response. I took a big sip to camouflage the sleepiness welling up inside my head, behind my eyes, then spun the straw noisily around in my glass, creating a little whirlpool.

"Maybe I'm just wondering, you know, why things never continue very long, and realizing there's nothing we can do about it. Maybe this is me giving up."

I nodded, made a noncommittal sound, and drank the last of my iced coffee.

A few months after she got pregnant, around the time her belly began to show, I started getting sleepy all the time. A thick fog of tiredness would form in the front of my brain, totally obscuring whatever had been on my mind a moment earlier—that month's credit card bill, the grading I still had to do, the crown that had come off my remaining left wisdom tooth. My eyelids would get heavier and heavier with each passing second, until I simply couldn't keep my eyes open. Heat spread from my palms up through my arms and on out from there, until my whole body felt warm, and I'd have a vision of someone slowly drawing a huge curtain before me, big enough to cover the sky. Nothing helped: not coffee, not washing my face. Even allocating time for an afternoon nap was no use. It reached the point where I was zoning out at work, and one of my colleagues got so annoyed he came to talk to me. "Yeah, I know," I told him. "I'm sleeping well enough, but I just get so damn tired. Maybe it's narcolepsy." He eyed me as I tried to make a joke of it, then grinned and said, "With what you've got, I don't think sleep will help." I didn't know what he was implying, but it was true: I had a sense this drowsiness wasn't something I could fix by sleeping more. It had come from somewhere unrelated to the everyday sort of sleepiness I was used to, and it was urging me toward some state altogether different from sleep.

The room the bellboy showed us to was on one of the upper floors; it wasn't too big, but it wasn't too small, either.

She glanced around contentedly and said the price seemed pretty cheap for such a nice room. Then: "Ugh, my legs are so swollen I can't move. Look at them."

We stuffed the suitcases in the closet without unpacking, then took off our shoes and put on the hotel slippers. She lay down on the bed, bent her legs, and pummeled away at her calves just like always, as if it were a ritual. Then she moved to the sofa, picked up the neatly folded newspaper from the table, and started reading it. Somewhere deep in my ears, I could still hear the dull slap of her hitting her calves. It wasn't exactly a slap or a whack—the sound was unlike any word I could pronounce, and it made me think of the dark, a rounded sort of darkness that was neither faint nor intense, just there. Then I found myself remembering the first time she told me to feel her belly: the firmness of that enormous swelling, a firmness that was like nothing else in the world, and how it stayed with me.

"They're bringing some pandas over," she said dully.

"Yeah, they were talking about it on TV the other day."

"They're talking about it in the newspaper, too."

She went back to the bed, leaned into the pillows heaped at the headboard, and began checking her messages on her cell phone.

"I always get annoyed watching pandas. I hate it when they eat bamboo."

"Why?"

"It feels like those leaves would shred your throat," she said.

"Well, it's not your throat," I said.

"Is there a rule saying I can't get annoyed unless it's my throat?"

I took a bottle of water out of the fridge, poured some into a glass, and drank. I turned on the TV and the word *Welcome* appeared, followed by a standard sort of welcome message and my name. I gazed blankly at the words for a while, and the screen switched to an ad for a massage service, then showed images of featured dishes at the restaurants. The screens kept popping up silently in sequence, again and again.

"When can we go back to Tokyo?" she asked eventually.

I sighed and looked over at her. We'd had this discussion any number of times. Without raising her eyes from her phone, she heaved an even louder sigh, as if to drown out mine.

"I don't know if I can take this anymore, unless there's a limit to how long we're staying. We've been there six months now, and I've seen all there is to see."

"I've told them that I'd like to be elsewhere," I said. "But there aren't many openings, and you know how hard it was just getting to the school I'm at now."

"What separates teachers who get positions in Tokyo from those who don't? Teachers who get what they request and teachers who don't?" she asked. "Is it luck?"

"Well, sort of," I replied. "It's all timing."

She stared at me for a while, looking like she was peering into a cave, then placed her cell phone on the nightstand, shook her head a little, and smiled. She slowly got up from the bed, making something of a display of how hard it was, massaged her hips, then peeled the covers down, lifted the sheets, and slid back into bed. I heard her mumble something, but I couldn't tell what it was.

I woke up at five.

Evidently I'd fallen asleep on the sofa. For a second I didn't know where I was, but after a few blinks I returned to my senses. I had sweated a lot as I slept, but by now my body was cool, and I felt a twinge of pain behind my eyes when I moved my head.

The bed seemed to levitate, white in the middle of the dimness of the room. I gazed at her where she lay wrapped in the covers; she was as still as a statue. The longer I stared at her form, made bulkier by the wrinkles and shadows of the fabric, the less human it looked. I started to feel as though maybe there wasn't anything under the covers at all. Maybe all there was under that white swelling was darkness. A hollow that would cave, just like that, if I pushed my fist into it.

I got up and walked over to the window, pulled the curtain, looked out at the city spread below me. The buildings, the rivers of cars, the sky—everything was sinking into that final dusky vagueness that comes just before the night paints everything black.

I flipped through the room service menu on the table. It had been more than six hours since we'd had lunch, and I was getting hungry, and yet somehow none of the pictures tempted me at all. I sat back down on the sofa, folded my arms, then stood up again and sat on the windowsill, watching as the lines of the buildings grew progressively less distinct, watching the colors of the darkening town. The air conditioner hummed quietly. A little later, her cell phone rang once, announcing the arrival of a text message. After that, it was silent.

I'm not sure how long I sat there. Eventually, sensing something behind me, I looked back and saw that she was looking at me from the bed. She was still wrapped up in the sheets; only her face was visible. Her wide-open eyes, clearly visible in the darkness, were staring straight into mine. I stared back at her for a moment, until she was awake enough to realize that she was looking at me.

"I had all these dreams," she said after some time, as if to herself. "All kinds."

Her tone of voice was very crisp, yet she didn't seem to have grasped that she was awake. She was alert, but some crucial part of her was swirling, muddy, and everything else about her was perfectly still. She just kept staring at me.

"About giving birth."

"Did you?"

"Our baby was born," she said. "It was yarn."

"Yarn?" I said, taken aback.

"Yes," she said quietly. "It was a world where everything was made of yarn. Water, people, train tracks, the ocean—all yarn. The ground, cups, clothes, date books. Things were knitted from this very soft, sturdy yarn. Everything. All yarn."

The room was darker than before; her face became dotted with odd little specks of color, as if it were being illuminated by a special sort of light. There weren't many spots; they were a color that could have been a very faint lavender or a very faint green. Where was the light coming from? Was it reflecting off something? I glanced around the room, but I couldn't identify the source.

"When something unpleasant or dangerous happens, things suddenly come apart. They go back to being just yarn, they wait it out."

"Interesting," I said.

"They're yarn, after all. Sometimes the yarn turns into sweaters, or mittens, and that's how they protect themselves. When something scares them, that's how they get through it."

"And our baby was yarn, too?"

"Yeah. It came straight out in a long line, as plain old yarn, and then when it was all out it sort of knitted itself into a baby shape, and I was the mother of a yarn baby. You were the father of yarn."

She didn't say anything after that. The silence continued for some time. I remembered that her cell phone had rung earlier and mentioned that, but she didn't respond.

"Even March was yarn," she said eventually.

"March?"

"Yeah. March."

"*March* was yarn?"

"That's right," she said. "In that world, even March was made of yarn."

"I don't think I get it," I said after a while.

"What's not to get?" she said.

"I can see how books and bags and stuff could be made out of yarn, but March isn't a thing, right? It's just a name we give to a segment of time. How can you make something like that out of yarn?"

She looked at me like I was talking nonsense. "I told you. In that world even March was made out of yarn."

"But what does that mean?" I said. "March is made out of yarn?"

"I told you. It means March is made out of yarn."

We lapsed into silence. Neither of us spoke for a while.

The silence then was total: the clock didn't tick, the air conditioner didn't hum. This was a bad sign. Whenever we stopped talking like this, I had to try to find a way to shift the topic as fast as I could. If I didn't toss out something specific that would elicit a specific response, we'd end up going through the same routine as always. And I was really not looking forward to that. We kept repeating the same thing again and again, and each time it got worse. This silence was the sign that we were heading into another tiresome back-and-forth.

I sighed, finished the water in my glass, and after a moment of hesitation started to tell her about a shirt I'd seen a foreign tourist wearing near Kiyomizu Temple. Before I could get into it, though, her cell phone rang. She slowly raised her upper body and reached to pick it up from the nightstand, only for it to stop ringing. She checked the screen and said she didn't know the number. She tried calling back, but there was no answer. She tried calling back a couple more times, but she couldn't get through—evidently the phone on the other end didn't even ring.

She looked up. "I had a message from Ono. She said she wanted to make sure we were okay after the earthquake."

"The earthquake?"

"That's what it says." She peered down at the screen.

"There was an earthquake?"

"I don't know, I guess there must have been."

"Was that her calling before?"

"I don't think so. I didn't recognize the number. . . . I wonder who it was. Strange."

"The reception is bad this high up. Try calling again later."

She thought a moment, then said that's what she'd do. After that she bundled herself up in the sheets and lay without moving.

"Hungry?" I asked. She didn't answer. I told her the hotel had all kinds of restaurants, and that if she wasn't feeling well we could order something from room service. I told her I'd noticed bouillabaisse on the menu. She didn't reply to that either. So I gave up, went over to the sofa, folded my arms, and closed my eyes.

✻

Some time later I heard her crying. I sighed silently and went and sat on the edge of the bed. The sky was a good deal darker than before, though I could still see long slivers of orange, piled in the west, just over the horizon. She lay sobbing for a while with her back to me. She started sniffling, so I took a few tissues from the box on the nightstand and held them, waiting as I always do for her to turn and face me.

It was a while before she spoke, and when she did her voice was hoarse.

"You saw that man bleeding . . . ?"

There was no light in the room by now, but still I could see the mucus glistening around her mouth.

"I saw him." I nodded, wiping her nose with the tissues.

"On the steps. Someone had to have punched him. He was bleeding so much, crouching there on the ground. I mean, he was an old man!"

"Yeah."

"I have no idea what happened, of course, but whatever it was, somebody hit him, a guy like that, a homeless guy, on those steps. There's no reason to hit a guy like him, he looked so weak, but someone obviously punched him. That's why there was so much blood."

"Who knows, maybe he just fell," I said tentatively.

She shook her head.

"It makes me so scared when I see things like that. People are such monsters. I'm not talking about specific people, just people in general—they're monsters. And I can't help it, I start thinking there's seriously no hope for this world, it's past saving. Someone gave birth to them too, you realize, that old man, and whoever beat him up, and eventually that's how it ends up, no matter how people want it to turn out. You go along living your life, and things happen, you get drawn into these things. Every day, day after day, there's always someone bleeding somewhere, and the only reason it hasn't been us yet is that our turn hasn't come. Maybe it's just not the right time yet, that's why we didn't bleed today, that's why we're here in this hotel. Maybe we were just lucky."

I took the wad of tissues, damp with tears and mucus, and dropped it in the trash. Then I took a few more and handed them to her.

"And much, much worse things can happen in this world. Things so awful you can't even imagine them. Is it really so wonderful to be born into a place like this? Is it? If we'd never been born, none of this would have existed, but we're here now, and now I have to—"

"Calm down."

"What if we're doing something terrible? Maybe this whole thing is a horrible mistake, so horrible it's beyond anything we've ever imagined, and it's already happening. Something we can never take back. Something truly awful. Maybe some awful future is waiting for us, and there's no turning back, and I'm about to start it all."

She covered her face with her hands and sobbed, her whole body shaking. I got into bed beside her and put my arms around her shoulders, told her it was okay.

"It's not all bad," I said. "There's a lot of bad in the world, but there's just as much good. Sure, there are guys who've been punched and bleed, and that's not going to stop, but not everyone's bleeding, you know."

She listened to my voice, pushing the tissues into her eyes.

"Besides, maybe he really did just fall."

"How come you're so optimistic?"

"I'm not optimistic, just noncommittal," I said. "I don't feel stuff in such an extreme way. I try not to think too hard about things that happen to me, and what I'm doing."

"Have you always been that way?"

"Always. It makes it easier."

She blew her nose loudly, then spent a long time rubbing her eyes with her palms. She lay on her back, rested her hands on either side of her bulging stomach, and stared at the ceiling, quietly trying to control her breathing.

"I said I don't like where we're living, but I did like that place we went the other day, with the boats shining all over the ocean, those boats, whatever they were."

"Squid boats. Firefly squid."

"The flags were beautiful. All those colors."

"They were."

"I'd like to go back."

"It's close enough, we can go as soon as we get home."

She nodded, then rested her head on my chest and stayed very still. Soon, as if the thought had just occurred to her, she whispered, "I'm so tired. I think I've caught what you have."

I told her she should get some rest, sleep as much as she could. As long as she wasn't hungry, she could sleep right now, and in the morning we'd get a nice breakfast.

"That sounds nice."

"Good night. We've got a long day tomorrow, so you better sleep well now."

Night had all but filled the room. A warm darkness had dissolved all the forms surrounding us, embracing us as we lay with our fingers locked together, like drifters with no hope of ever settling anywhere. She was sound asleep. Peering at her, I saw that her swollen belly was hovering a few centimeters above the bed, rising and falling like a ball floating on the waves. A single piece of yarn was climbing from the area around her belly button, higher and higher, like a living creature with a will of its own, and little by little the skin there was coming undone. I watched, feeling myself begin to crumble into sleep. Here, right at this moment, all the different sleeps people were sleeping, all across the world, had started spinning slowly into whirlpools that flowed gently into one another, combined into a vast swell that was pushing us, and our hotel room, toward a place neither of us had ever seen. I knew what I needed to do: I had to hold tight to the bed and lean out over the edge, try to see what was at the center of the whirlpool. But my eyelids felt so heavy, and my hands were coming undone; there was no strength in them now. I heard a phone ringing in the distance. It kept ringing and ringing, like a voice calling after someone, trying to keep him from leaving. Seventeen times, twenty-one times—still it rang. I gave up counting and closed my eyes, sure that this time, this time, I would make it all the way down to the bottom.

LULU

Shinji Ishii

Translated by Bonnie Elliott

Ever since that day, Lulu had been seeing the translucent women descend each evening.

An icy grayness spread across the cold concrete floor in the large room where foldout cots were propped up unceremoniously side by side. Fitful snores eased into the tranquil hum of sleep escaping from under pale blue sheets, only to be interrupted by the grinding of teeth, heavy groans, and the echo of screams that could rip through a swollen throat. Nobody dared to wake up.

During the day, the children spent most of their time in silence watching things come and go, the endless paperwork, the strangers sitting across from them, attempting to counsel. In the evening, once they lay down in their separate cots, they seemed undoubtedly animated as they mumbled into the darkness. The sound, however, was not of their voices. It was the rasp of different realities knocking into one another. There was nothing that resembled the sound of conversations held anywhere else under the sun communicating intentions and thought; yet the noise was without a doubt authentic, emitted by each child in their own way, ringing true only to themselves in that very moment, in that very room, breathing in that darkness. At first, Lulu thought that the women were drawn to this room by the purity of these voices.

Something seemed to be stirring near the ceiling. Through half-open eyes, Lulu saw streams of light come pouring down, as if a curtain of rain. Lulu raised her body off the floor to stare at the light and the translucent women floating through it. Hovering above the cots, with a gentle smile on their faces, they extended rainbow-hued arms and caressed the pale cheeks of the children, patted their heads, and softly stroked their near-crumpled backs.

Lulu did not dare bark. She held her breath, careful not to snort or pant. The translucent women did not turn toward Lulu. It could have been because Lulu was hidden, huddled in the shadow of the cabinet, or perhaps the women chose not to acknowledge her. Lulu's tail, which often wagged unambiguously, seemed lost in thought, moving quietly to and fro. The sight of floating translucent women was far from anything Lulu was used to, so she was feeling uncertain. In this light, for those in the room, what had just befallen the land and altered its landscape seemed to prepare them for any and all possibilities.

Lulu had no idea how long the translucent women had been floating above the children. In fact, the concept of time, in minutes or hours, was unknown to Lulu.

Sleep did not enter her mind.

Twisting their bodies slightly, the translucent women rose higher before being absorbed into the light, an outline of their bodies clear, then disappearing in the darkness, rather like a candle burning brightest before going out. It was only after the last woman disappeared that Lulu became aware of the lull in the room. The air was as still as if at the bottom of a lake. Gone were the painful grunts and groans from the children. It was hard to believe that the room was ever filled with their piercing cries. In fact, the gentle sounds of sleep escaping the children's lips gathered in the darkness, like bubbles frothing around kelp, and rose upward to bump against the ceiling and shower the room with serenity. This continued until the morning sun shone through the frosted glass windows. As Lulu watched the first child sit up in bed, then the second and the third, she finally laid her head down and drifted into a restless sleep.

The women returned that evening and the next. They flowed out from intertwined rays of white light along the ceiling, descending to hover above the cots and caress each sleeping child's tired face. The ordinarily dingy ceiling spar-kled like the silver surface of a lake. The women must come from a city of weightlessness, Lulu thought, and perhaps that was why they were able to float between time and space, reaching out to the children and giving them the gift of rest far flung from this land. While keeping an eye on the river of light, Lulu walked across the floor as quietly as possible. She did not need to turn to the women to know they were watching her; she could smell it. Even among dogs, whose sense of smell was 100 million times sharper than humans', Lulu's was superior, and that was why she had been, on that unforgettable day, assaulted by a frenzied wave with the stench of dread so intense it almost ripped her to shreds. But tonight, Lulu soaked in the scents showered from above and was transported to springtime, running across a grassy field without a leash. Light laughed and danced around the room, fluttering like butterflies. Lulu realized that the women were talking to the children. Freed from the constraints of gravity, they spoke in the language of light, which was not heard as a voice but as layers of color spreading through the mind. So that the children saw rather than listened.

The children were sometimes replaced by others. There were some that disappeared for a few days only to return clutching tightly to their belongings. The face would seem normal, eyes and nose set correctly, but the suffering and pain had the effect of turning the countenance into a tangled mess of hair. One of the translucent women hovered above a boy lying as still as a sandbag and extended her arm toward him. She began disentangling his mess, strand by strand, while a quiet breeze carried kindness from her center toward him. After a few nights, the boy started to sleep calmly, the tangled mess in his heart given comfort. The women seemed to be reaching out to the children night after night, fully aware of each child's story. Perhaps it was not too long ago that the women had experienced something similar themselves. They made no lament, and instead beamed their smiles with quiet light, their voices blanketing the children with tranquility.

Lulu walked among the cots without making a sound. It was difficult for her to make out the features of the women because of their translucence, but Lulu knew from the scents and the air around them that there were many different women. Nor would the same woman tend to the same child each evening. It seemed that these women were free-spirited and whimsical.

As she circled the room, Lulu came to realize one thing: there were some sleeping children whom the women did not visit. Never were these children touched or spoken to. Lulu held her breath, lifted her head, and walked down the aisle. She was never good with numbers but began counting this one and that one: there were three boys and two girls, of varying ages, each a hardened mass curled up in bed. No noise came from them. No grinding of teeth, no groans, not even a rustle of the sheets. They were enveloped in a deep, dark sleep. Lulu peered up at the women as if to plead for their attention, but they were each, with arms extended, attending other children, incapable of lifting their heads to acknowledge these five others.

Lulu placed her paws on the cot in front of her and swiftly sprung up onto it. The sheets felt crisp. This unattended boy appeared foglike in ash, curled into a ball like a roly-poly bug. After gazing at the boy, who was sleeping on his side, Lulu confirmed the slow rise and fall of his shoulders, but the boy emitted no smell of sweat—it was as though he had been wrung dry.

She rubbed her nose against the back of the boy's T-shirt and licked his neck. It felt like stone. She stepped over the boy to face him and stared at his blank expression. Slowly she began to follow the example of the women, touching the boy's cheeks with gentle strokes. She rubbed her fur on him, tensing her throat and making certain each spot of the boy's downy face was touched and tickled with care. In time, there was a change. It began with a something like a bubble popping. Then breath that emerged as quietly as a tide ebbing on a distant shore. Lulu fought the urge to move her chin up and down and instead tried to duplicate what the women were doing with their fingers. She concentrated on rhythmically, ever so softly, stroking the boy's cheeks, which were bathed in light. After the small bursts of breath continued, the boy's lips opened to release a noise akin to a fully inflated bellows that had been suddenly stepped on with brute force. The hair around Lulu's chin stiffened, then dog and child snuggled and laughed. Deep breaths the boy had been holding back were expelled all at once, spreading across the ceiling like specks of snow and scattering and melting in the dark. The translucent women, hearing the commotion, looked at one another, then looked at Lulu, who continued her rhythmic stroking of the boy's cheeks. They then tossed out the gentlest of smiles, shaped much like a lotus blossom, toward Lulu.

That evening was spent solely on the boy. The next day Lulu, nodding in and out of sleep, kept watch over the children and their adult caretakers. She slipped behind the cabinet in the early evening to wait for night and the arrival of the translucent women. As a lull descended over the room, Lulu stared wide-eyed as a pillar of light seemed to burst through the ceiling and melt into the moonlight coming through the windows, flowing together as a river of light. The women were already floating above the children, flickering in the evening light. There were more women tonight, not just above the cots but also playfully gathering above the dish carts and folded stretchers. Lulu trotted over to the boy from the night before. He was curled into a ball again, but feeling Lulu's fur against his cheek, he lifted his chin to throw out a lump of breath from the base of his throat, and as though he had just been uncorked, began to take repeated breaths, regularly and calmly. Here and there along the ceiling, the women began to take notice.

Lulu headed toward a dark corner of the room where a girl, who hardly moved during the day, lay in bed. Because there were hardly any signs of her presence in the air, it took a while for Lulu to confirm her existence. When Lulu first climbed onto the cot, although the girl was under the sheets, instead of a rounded shape that protruded, there was a concave indentation. The sheets were but a prop to hide the wide-open, dark hole that lay beyond. Lulu instinctively heard an echo warning her not to lift the sheets. Once you set foot under, the voice said, you will cease to be yourself.

Chills ran up Lulu's spine. She was about to retreat when unexpectedly she was overtaken by another, more emphatic voice that rang through her heart: NO, THAT'S NOT IT! Lulu stood paralyzed. Suddenly, in her mind's eye, she saw what she and her siblings had gone through soon after they were born. It was as if a long and thin arm extended out from the past, waving a colored photograph in her face. The screeching, the flames, the smell of gasoline, the odor of her mother's bodily fluids. Images of a slippery white floor she was thrown out onto, and the endless hours spent in isolation.

After slipping out between glass doors, Lulu spent years eating whatever she could find, including grass and paper. She had a limp in her right hind leg and her back had dozens of scars from black kites gouging her. One day when she was drinking from a puddle near the pipes outside the municipal children's facility, she heard a metallic tapping, then saw something with a dull shine being placed on the ground. Lulu lifted her gaze and walked toward it. In an aluminum bowl there was a muddy brown mix of stuff. She took one nervous lick, then immediately stuck her mouth into the bowl to devour what was there. Dressed in a white coat and carrying a ladle, the Lunch Lady smiled at Lulu. The muddy brown mix in the dish, Lulu learned later, was "doggy chow," and the Lunch Lady made it with rice and miso soup and water to cut down on the sodium.

Until that day, Lulu had been, without a doubt, a dog with a gaping hole. She would willingly plunge headfirst into that hole and get ripped to shreds but would find herself standing on the street again, where she would be forced to jump back into that dark hole, enduring a life of endless repetition. But the Lunch Lady poured something warm into that hole, allowing Lulu to experience, for the first time in her life, an infusion of flavor and light, which she felt with every cell of her body.

Lulu took a look at the sheets again. She sensed that her sitting here at this very moment was a promise she had made a long time ago: she was meant to be here on the cot where the girl with the dark hole lay. Lulu stuck her nose under the sheets and sniffed her way toward the concave girl and came to her back. She snuggled up close and tight.

After a slow, burning silence, Lulu was overtaken by a scream that blazed like hellfire through her body. She used all her might to resist the pull into the dark hole. This sound was neither human nor animal. It was a voice born after life is given up on; it was a voice that cast a black spell on all living things. Lulu dangled, clinging to the edge of the hole, as the furious wind of the scream whipped her, destroying pieces of her body. She could not imagine what had happened to the girl; she did not want to know. Lifting her gaze above the sonic waves of the scream, she saw the women, who had earlier been floating playfully near the ceiling, looking at her with half-smiles on their faces. It was a kind of half-smile that understood about giving up on something and allowing the self to be turned inside out many times over. Lulu, being turned inside out, let go and fell backward into the hole, toward the screaming voice. In the darkness, images from the end of the world appeared and disappeared. Lulu understood: this was what the girl experienced on that day. Lulu understood that it was only the beginning.

The girl's shrieks smashed scenes from the end of the world to bits. As Lulu fell deeper into the hole, the force tore off a leg, broke her neck, and trampled her guts. Yet she had no intention of offering herself up to the girl. What was going through her mind was the Lunch Lady. This woman served hundreds of aluminum bowls of food with her ladle, always with a belly laugh. With one hand she tossed Lulu leftovers whenever there were any. The Lunch Lady looked to be no more than thirty in human years. Lulu wanted to be like the Lunch Lady. If only she could fill this hole with light and color, she prayed. If only she could accomplish this task, the Lunch Lady would be the first person to rejoice and laugh from deep in her heart.

Lulu could taste the warmth of that first meal from the Lunch Lady. As she continued to be turned inside out, flowing in and out of herself, she threw that same warmth out into the spiraling, shrieking void. Lulu's physical body ceased to exist; in its place a hollow effigy of her former body served as a medium to keep the memory of true warmth alive. The sound of the Lunch Lady's ladle tapping the aluminum bowl echoed through the space where rising steam morphed into the faces of the many little ones gathered in the cafeteria, each with a smile on their face. The shrieks began to die down. As did the groans and grinding of teeth. But the one sound that echoed off the walls of the room was the sound of someone gurgling as they struggled to fight rising floodwaters. Before she knew it, Lulu stepped over the girl, but what really happened was that she had pushed through the dark hole and emerged on the other side. There she was, huddled in a ball by the girl's chest, looking right at her. Gently she licked the tears rolling down the girl's cheeks. Both Lulu and the girl were soaked to the bone, as if they had just been pulled from ocean waters. Whether Lulu pulled the girl out of the rising tide or whether the girl had pulled Lulu out was unclear. Perhaps they had pulled together as one.

The translucent women hovered above the cot, whispering to one another in the language of light like celestial birds. The little girl held Lulu close, petting her as though her life depended on this exact movement, and in response, Lulu fluffed out her chest and let the girl continue. The tears on the girl's peach-tinted cheeks tasted like the salt-dipped green apples that the Lunch Lady sometimes tossed to Lulu.

The following night, Lulu visited her third and fourth child, pulling each of them out of darkness and back into the land of peaceful sleep. She flung herself into holes and traveled to motionless dark depths where she melded with the little ones, shrieking gutturally, then floated outward and upward toward the beckoning grains of light to emerge on the pale blue sheets. Sometimes she had to try more than once. Lulu waited for the right moment, her churning chest tense, before casting her body out of the hole. Fueled by the shrieks and wind, Lulu searched for the child's most calming memory—flickering birthday candles, holding hands and jumping down a set of stairs at the park, the smile of parents—even as she gave herself up to the scream and threw herself down the hole. Lulu always found herself soaking wet on the sheets, being hugged by a convulsively crying child. After she caught her breath, she began to enjoy being patted unrelentingly by each child and reveled in the sensation of returning the favor. Up near the ceiling, the many translucent women smiled tenderly. Lulu did not know that her body was slowly losing its outline and that, little by little, she was becoming invisible.

The fifth child was a girl who had lost her sight on that day. Her field of vision was locked in darkness and home to a thick iridescent stream overflowing with sensory experiences. Her cracked, dehydrated body twitched in silence—this was her guttural scream. Lulu did not feel the urge to run from these sounds anymore. She opened her entirety to the scream, letting some of it flow out, finally melding into the girl's body to be caught up in the massive orbit that took them where they needed to go. Most important was the fact that this girl was alive. It was the reason they were allowed entry into the flowing circle. More than the millions of unreachable lights in the heavens, this dimly flickering light, however small, was truly what kept the world illuminated. The girl opened her eyes quietly and let one sparkling teardrop, then another, fall onto the dry sheets. And then alongside fragments of memory, parts of her hardened soul crumbled in a gushing torrent of tears.

When Lulu awoke hugged tightly by the little girl, it was the first time she did not recognize where she was. The outline of Lulu's body had all but vanished, her feet were waffling in search of the floor, and her eyes could not distinguish up from down nor left from right. After blinking a few times, Lulu realized that she had completely lost her eyesight, too. She heard voices from above that sounded like rustling leaves, and before she knew it, her body lifted up from the sheets and slowly floated upward.

A scent seemed to itch her nose, jogging her memory. It smelled of a time and place with her siblings, how they rolled in a meadow until they were deep in grass on a land they called home. The scent expanded, spreading gentle ripples of laughter across the room. Arms reached out as Lulu's body levitated. They stroked her cheeks and tickled her chin. She lifted her sightless eyes toward the all-embracing scent. She laughed out loud. She knew without a doubt that the Lunch Lady was up here, at one with the translucent women and the deliciously golden fragrance.

Twelve years passed. Though unusual, a reunion of the thirty-two children who had slept in the same large room in that municipal children's facility had been organized.

In a ballroom at a hotel on a hill in town, the organizer, a pediatrician who had just begun his residency at the university hospital, made a brief speech, then raised his beer glass in a toast to the occasion. The response was a chorus of cheers, followed by applause.

The organizer was not the only one in the group who worked in the town. In fact, he was but one of many, including several who were students at the university or vocational schools. It was as though they were embraced by the land of their birth. In spite of the mounds of debris still littering the harbor and foothills of the landscape devastated that day, the town had undergone a steady recovery over the decade, and for the thirty-two people who gathered at the hotel, the townscape mirrored their own journey.

Nobody in the room could have imagined the possibility of such devastation had that day not occurred. In a parallel world, a completely different future lay waiting for them, and they would be wearing different shoes, sitting across from different people. Though burdened by such worries, they were truly alive on this very day, and seeing one another was reason to rejoice. Indeed, all thirty-two had recovered enough to appreciate this fact. As long as they were alive, they had no choice but to keep moving forward at whatever pace possible, for everyone had done just that. But it was clear that in the twelve years it would normally take a child to grow into adulthood, these thirty-two adults had acquired the knowledge and life experience of people well beyond their years.

Among the group were two couples who had married in the last two years. One of the women held a nine-month-old baby in a sling, and the other sat at a table eating a plate of Chinese food while she rubbed her round belly.

As if to fill a lull in the conversation, the pediatrician, with an impish smile, asked the young construction worker, "You remember, right, that we had a dog?"

This caused the construction worker to think back for a moment. He then chortled before replying, "Oh yeah, you're right, we did have a dog."

"Hey, what are you guys talking about?" a young woman asked, approaching the two men. She was famous as a hostess at the local pub where the construction worker and many others in the room were regulars.

"Yoko, you were too little to remember," said the construction worker. "We had a dog in that big room. It wasn't old, but it wasn't a puppy. It was a smart dog."

"Man, was that a good dog."

The conversation was soon joined by others, each of whom shared a memory with a twinkle in their eyes:

"We'd tell it to go find us slippers or mittens, and it would do just that."

"Didn't bark."

"But it barked at that fat counselor," the young mother added.

"For real. Totally."

"Didn't poop," said the slightly drunk postman, who then laughed. "Didn't pee and didn't eat, either."

The pediatrician, smiling uncomfortably at Yoko, explained: "In other words, we were pretending to have a dog."

It was unclear who had come up with the idea. Because animals were not allowed at the facility, no one was allowed to bring a pet from home. Not that many of the children had homes to begin with. Then someone got the idea that they would keep a dog that only the children would know about. The children created a daily schedule for walks and meals. No adult would be able to see the dog, but it would live and play openly with them in the big room.

"In other words, an 'air dog.'"

"Air . . . dog . . ." Yoko repeated with wide-open eyes.

The older ones recalled that in the morning, the child who'd been on duty during the night handed the leash over to the next child on duty, reporting on what the dog had done that night. Stories were plentiful: it learned to fetch the rubber ball from the corners of the room, it stared intently at the door to make sure nothing suspicious entered the room, it was bitten on the nose by a mosquito and looked ready to cry, it ran and played outside in the snow for what seemed like forever . . . The color of its fur changed from brown to black according to who was on duty, and it fattened like a calf or slimmed down to a toy breed. Its favorite food, the mix of rice and miso soup called "doggy chow," was introduced by a boy whose grandfather, a gardener, had had a dog. Somehow this became the go-to meal for whoever was on duty, and it quickly replaced the semimoist dog food that was the original meal of choice. There were special touches, of course, like using less salt or sprinkling in some dried sardines, and with their combined effort everyone agreed that the "air dog" was looking generally healthier than before.

"When it first wandered in, it looked like a skinny stray, but then it took a liking to the Lunch Lady."

Nobody knew anything about where the Lunch Lady from the cafeteria had been at that very moment or what kind of hell overtook her on that day. Nor did they know what had become of her since. Like clockwork, at lunch each day she had ladled vegetable soup into aluminum bowls. The Lunch Lady did let slip that she would be making a special dinner of fried shrimp and crab risotto in celebration of two birthdays—Yoko's and someone else's—on that day. A couple of older people in the group, who were teenagers back then, remembered this clearly.

Before coming to the children's facility, the Lunch Lady had been working at the restaurant her family owned. She was the kind of woman who had the sweetest smiles for the children, and when it came to cooking, she did not compromise on a single ingredient, so everyone was looking forward to the birthday dinner. Since she had a tight budget, it was likely that she would have gone to the riverbank by the harbor to acquire on her own what she needed.

"That dog waited for the Lunch Lady's return for days."

"Really?" mumbled a young man who was studying to be an accountant. "I seem to remember that we started having the dog after the Lunch Lady disappeared."

"That's impossible," said the postman. "If the dog came on that day, how could it have gotten close to the Lunch Lady, who worked at the cafeteria before that day?"

The accounting student thought about this for a moment. "So perhaps . . ." he said, swallowing as he noticed the silence in the room, "it only goes to show that he was really an air dog to begin with."

"What are you talking about?! I definitely remember the Lunch Lady giving us lessons on how to make doggy chow!" the mother exclaimed as her baby wiggled in the sling.

The accounting student was a lanky young man with digestive problems. Had the postman or the pediatrician, who were four or five years his senior, persisted in the argument, he would likely have crumbled. But this student had, no less than the others, lived the twelve years since that day as best he could, accepting his fate and choosing to move forward on his own two feet. He really didn't want to be the agitator. He just felt the need to figure out one thing about the dog that he may have been alone in questioning. It was against the rules, he thought, to keep silent, and he had to relay it to the others with whom he shared the big room. He understood this not with his mind but with his whole body.

"Honestly, I don't remember the lessons on making doggy chow," said the young man as he looked directly at people gathered around. "The Lunch Lady was an adult, no?"

The pediatrician let out a gasp. "Is it possible that even though she was an adult, she had the power to see the dog? I kind of remember that we were pretty darn strict with the rules."

Nobody said a word. Had the Lunch Lady not seen the dog? Is that to say the dog ran up to, was fed by, and got close to someone that couldn't see it? But then could the dog see the Lunch Lady? In the aftermath of that day, had the dog and the Lunch Lady both run backward with such fervor that they ran weeks into the past and met by the pipes outside the facility with nothing but an aluminum bowl between them? Were they both invisible when they met?

"So much has happened, hasn't it?" the woman with the round belly said softly. She was entering her eighth month of pregnancy. "That day and even afterward, it feels like so much happened at the same time. I can't really remember when we started taking care of that dog either. But you know what, if it was something we couldn't see, it should be free to exist in many ways. I mean, after all, its size and breed changed freely."

Relief showed on everyone's face. After some nods, stories about the air dog spilled out, about the times when each child had been on dog duty. Its health and fur, its expressions and mannerisms, its funny habits—all were told one after another. Beer was poured with abandon, and the air in the room mixed with a golden light that slowly encompassed all in it. It soon became apparent that each person there who remembered the air dog so vividly had real dogs of their own in their new lives. And although none of them realized it, their real dogs were replicas of this air dog.

"You know," the somewhat inebriated construction worker said, turning to Yoko, "I've been thinking, but the name of the dog, you know, I can't remember it. What was it?"

"How would I know?" said Yoko, scrunching her shoulders.

"Man, I can't remember if there was a name we all used or if we all had different names for it."

Among the thirty-two at this gathering, there were five who seemed to stay away from the conversation at this table, keeping their lips sealed shut, sitting elsewhere. At first, out of consideration, the others brought plates of food over to them, but the task of holding a conversation with them proved too difficult and the five were soon left on their own. From the vantage point of the group, these five seemed to be engaged in separate activities, blankly staring at the wall or gazing at the clock, but in fact they had just begun to intone the same word over and over again in their hearts.

These five were the only ones who traveled from afar to attend the reunion. After leaving the center, they were unable to find a school or workplace in town that was willing to take them on. They were estranged from one person to the next until, finally reaching a place that offered no sense of belonging, they slipped right through junior high school and landed jobs that did not require human contact. Their current circumstances differed, but the bitterness of feeling thrown out of their place of birth bound them together. Even so, all five took numerous trains to return to this town so they could, in the guise of a reunion, stand atop this land to call out the name repeating in their hearts:

Lulu.
Lulu, Lulu.
Lulu, Lulu, Lulu.

It wasn't that the five of them got together to name the dog Lulu. Then again, perhaps all thirty-two of them had been calling the dog Lulu. But here in the corner of the ballroom, the five who were repeating the dog's name as if in prayer had an intense emotional tide, absent from the other twenty-seven, swirling within them.

Lulu was *not* an invisible, imaginary dog.

Each remembered the exact sensation of fur tickling their foreheads and the soft spot under their chins. They remembered the breath that smelled of grass and the weight of her jaw, which was heavier than it looked. In that big room, the dog appeared just as the darkness of night descended heavily upon them; it jumped onto their cots and slipped right into their hearts like a missing puzzle piece, staying right by their faces until they fell asleep. Had Lulu not been there, one said, I would have been a crumpled wreck in the corner of that dimly lit room. Assaulted and shredded by the wave, washed to the land of nowhere, I would have sunk to the dark ocean floor, another said. Yes, one agreed. Lulu's fur was incredibly soft, but it was the world's warmest and strongest lifesaver, one added. With Lulu by my side, I could sail through the angriest waves in the roughest seas, said the fifth.

Lulu.
Lulu, Lulu.
Lulu, Lulu, Lulu.

This sense of security was not confined to the big room at the children's facility. It was felt in a dormitory in a never-heard-of town, at a neon-lit countryside inn, a rust-ridden apartment. When poked fun at, stepped on, or ignored. Even during times that they did not feel vulnerable, as soon as the lights were turned off, when the darkness became a wave, a thick wall, slamming into them, sweeping them into turbulence, into the depths of darkness. At those times, Lulu never failed to appear. But she did not visit as she did twelve years ago, when she would jump up onto their cots. She now appeared bathed in light, slowly descending from the shimmering blue ceiling. When she snuggled against their chests and panted, her breath carried the scent of grass and miso soup. Lulu visited last night, too. Lulu, you're here today, aren't you?

Eventually these five found their gazes lifted to a spot near the cream-colored ceiling where light appeared to float. Beyond the gentle sway spread a meadow of light where a dog dashed through the grass. As if after a rain shower, each blade of grass shimmered and danced in the wind. The dog ran with its tongue lapping at the air and it was surely smiling. The air filled with the scent of sweet memories, and soon the meadow was home to many similar-looking dogs, panting heavily and somehow lined up in a row. The dog beamed even brighter as it kicked its legs up, running like a ray of light across the plain.

In the meadow stood a small house. Wisps of cottony smoke rose from the chimney, spreading the aroma of a simmering stew. In a bravado of weightlessness, the dog skipped through the air and rolled toward the house.

Just because you cannot see something doesn't mean it

isn't there. Between two beings who were invisible, the ability to see each other in the reflection of one another's invisibility was imaginable and even possible. For the five who sat apart from the group, the smell of the dirt of the land beneath them, intact for the past twelve, one hundred, ten thousand years, rose swiftly and filled the room to connect all things seen and unseen.

Soon the twenty-seven others were also looking up at the ceiling. The pediatrician, construction worker, young mother, accounting student, Yoko, and the woman who was eight months pregnant were all squinting and sniffing as they observed the faintly lit island of space above as though they were gazing at a clear sky seen through a hole in the ceiling. Sunlight showered like rain upon each of the thirty-two faces.

In the meadow, the dogs played boisterously, yelping and dashing about. Smiles of light sparkled, dancing and fluttering like butterflies. The wooden door of the house swung open and out stretched a hand clutching a ladle waving to and fro, calling to the children and dogs, beckoning them all to step into the house.

ONE YEAR LATER

J. D. McClatchy

In this photograph
He is knee-deep in water,
Half-smiling, half-scared.

His cracked Transformer,
His knapsack, his cup, his cat.
Why did they survive?

How is it we leave so much
Behind for others to touch?

*

Ministers, tell me,
Why did you think that power
Would stay where it was?

Aging cores collapse
Under waves of a future
No one can live in.

The reactors stand there still.
What is left to warm or kill?

                    *

The news crawl's moved on
To other smaller, larger,
Distant disasters.

Get on with your life,
A shy inner voice insists
On the crowded screen.

Our lives lengthen into death,
As if into one last breath.

                    *

He watched for too long.
He could not run fast enough.
He was lifted up

With all the others
Into reruns of the day
No one's come back from.

When I took that photograph
He was seven and a half.

GRANDMA'S BIBLE

Natsuki Ikezawa

Translated by Alfred Birnbaum

The trees straight ahead shine especially bright. Sure, it's the season for new foliage, but since when were the leaves so luxuriant? Could almost squeeze a cool jade-green gleam out of them. Must be something wrong with my eyes.

"The next shelter is back in the hills a bit," Satomura informs me. "Take a left up there."

I veer off onto a side grade, which angles down to a rocky streambed. Keeping an eye to the coastal flats strewn with rubble, I turn left and pass under the main road we were on to parallel the stream up into the hills. The rubble soon disappears.

We drive on for maybe fifteen minutes.

"The car feels lighter," I say.

"Made some runs this morning, so there's less load."

The road forks off again to the left, away from the stream and up a slight incline. Several houses appear by the roadside. A tiny settlement, but not a soul in sight. As I steer between the houses, a larger lodge comes into view on high. I pull up in front and ease to a stop.

"Tadanuma Community Center," reads the large wooden plaque. Tacked up beside it someone has written "Tadanuma Shelter" on a piece of paper, sunburned and frayed at the edges. It's been three months now.

We get out and go around to open the hatchback. Not many supplies left. We open a few boxes, half expecting people to show when they hear the car, but there's not a sound. The men might be out clearing away rubble, but womenfolk generally stay around, minding the chores and odd jobs and kids.

"Hello! Anybody there? Mr. Taneyama?" shouts Satomura, reading from his memo pad. "He's our contact here," he explains to me.

No answer. The people aren't just off somewhere; they're gone by the look of it.

"Guess everybody must've moved."

"To temp housing? News to me."

"Hello?" Satomura shouts even louder into the doorway. "Anybody around?"

We're just about to head back to the car when a man appears in the distance from behind the building. We wave at him. He quickens his step, but seems in no special hurry to make his way down to us in the front yard. He's carrying a handful of plants of some kind.

"I'm Satomura from the Emishi Relief Team. I've been here before."

"You volunteers?" asks the man. Fiftyish, but lean with a healthy posture. Somehow that makes him look a little citified, though his worn-out work pants and plain sweatshirt are no different than anyone else's.

"Yeah, from the Emishi Relief Team," repeats Satomura, but he gets no reaction. "We've come to deliver relief goods. Is Mr. Taneyama not around?"

"They've all gone. Moved to temp housing yesterday, already had the closing ceremony. I'm orphaned here to tidy things up."

Orphaned. His overblown choice of words is novel, oddly comical.

"Well then, guess you won't be needing anything here. No towels or toilet paper or kids' summer clothes or sunblock or dust masks?" Satomura almost sounds like a traveling salesman.

"Don't need anything here, but the folks in the temps probably will. Leave things with me and I'll ferry them over."

"Where are these temp quarters?"

"In three different places. We told them we didn't want to be split up, but bureaucracy does what it does."

"Okay, what do you say we leave you some stuff?"

The man nods, so Satomura and I quickly throw together a few items in a cardboard box.

"Anything particular in short supply? The women mention anything?"

Ask male leaders at most relief shelters and they'll say they've got everything they need. Ask the women in secret so as not to make the men lose face, and hesitatingly (though at great length) they'll tell you all the things they need. Women live closer to reality—it's their role to bear.

"I did hear something about cosmetics."

Luckily, we have some in our load. Leftover samples of facial moisturizer donated by a major manufacturer. I'm sorting these out of the larger boxes when I happen to say, "Why not leave *that* here too?"

"*What?* The sake?"

We'd been loading surplus goods at a warehouse in the next prefecture when a helping hand pressed a great big one-*sho* bottle on us. "Take this, too, if you think somebody'd want it. The sake's three years old, so the taste may have turned," the guy said.

We huddle in whispers, then hand over the bottle along with the caution.

The man accepts it with a smile. "Haven't we met somewhere?" he asks to my face.

"Hmm, not that I can remember," I answer, returning his gaze.

"Oh, c'mon. I'm dead sure we've met."

Okay, supposing we had, what difference would that make? Why not just say we met here and now? We'll be going our separate ways soon enough.

"You a volunteer too?"

"Yeah, a volunteer driver on weekends."

I'm thinking I want to get out of here quick.

"Thanks for the goods," he says. "I'm Kensaku Kimura."

"My name's a little tricky. Written *kara* and *ushi*, pronounced 'Karoji,'" I tell him in exchange. Satomura had already introduced himself up front.

The man, however, gives no reaction. No sign of prior recognition.

"Make good use of all that," I say, gesturing toward the box of items we've left on the doorstep as I make for the driver's seat.

This Kimura just stands there with a blank look. Then he takes a single step. A fathomless expression floats up from deep under the surface.

"You all busy after this?" he asks.

"Got one more drop-off. Then it's on to Tohno Dorm, which is a fair haul."

The man obviously wants to speak. Is he so very starved for company? His assurances that we've met merely a twisted indication of that longing? Whatever, he seems to recognize something familiar in me.

"Nah, I just thought maybe we could talk a bit," he says.

It's not uncommon for us to hear out what people at relief shelters have to say. Even the most tightlipped souls who view us warily at first will suddenly start talking nonstop.

Okay, I'm all ears.

I shoot Satomura a knowing look and before I can change my mind I say, "I'll stay on and hitch a ride back to Tohno tomorrow."

Our Kimura shines with a shy grin. "There's still some food rations left . . . and your sake too."

But why me and not Satomura? It's not just our similar ages, is it? He's sensed a more tragic scent here.

I turn to face him. "Let's drink on it."

"Sure, okay," seconds Satomura. "Or I could come back around after the Tohno run."

"No, that's too far to go. I'll be okay. I'll be in touch tomorrow."

And at that, Satomura heads off.

"I'm from around these parts," the man tells me. "Not from Tadanuma, from Matsubetsu on the coast."

Matsubetsu has been leveled flat by the tsunami. Nothing there now but rubble. The same goes for everywhere two hundred kilometers north or south of here, of course. And so begins a night of drinking.

Three years hasn't affected the sake much, and there are cans of things to eat. Also some odd Chinese instant seafood congee. You're supposed to put it in a bowl, add hot water, and wait five minutes, but we pass on it and start drinking. A one-*sho* bottle between the two of us should be plenty. Anyway, there's not a liquor store for ten kilometers in any direction.

He's from Matsubetsu, Kimura tells me, but he lived there only until he was six, when he was taken in by relatives in Tokyo due to family circumstances. By the time he came back up to Tohoku during high school, his parents were dead. The only family he had left was a much older brother and his young wife, who was a town clerk. An okay life, he had to admit.

After that he'd show up in his estranged hometown every couple of years. His brother's store was doing a steady business, the two kids growing without any major hitch. He himself had graduated from university in engineering and taken a job with an electrical firm, though not in manufacturing—he became a "sales engineer." (I, too, have a degree in science, I mention in passing.) He married a woman he met through work; they had no children, but otherwise they were happy enough.

Eventually he launched his own venture, marketing his old company's wind-powered generator equipment, mainly to overseas clients, and moved sufficient volume to support twenty employees.

Life was good; then two years ago something happened: his wife wanted to leave him for another man. Discussions and arguments dragged on, but in the end he gave in. Once there's a crack in the relationship, there's no holding it together for long. Less painful for both simply to let their story end. The mortgage was paid up, so she got the condo and he rented a small place for himself. He let go of the better half of their possessions, gave her whatever she asked for, disposed of the rest. He'd never been very attached to things anyway.

Next came a shakeup at the office. His trusted vice-director from years back joined forces with another concern and skillfully maneuvered him out of the CEO chair.

"So there I was, having to come up with a whole new life at age fifty," he says, paper cup of sake in hand.

Well, these things happen. There are times you find yourself in such straits you don't even have the strength to imagine a different possibility. One day he nearly punched out a joker who made a callous remark about incompetent volunteers.

"Can eat only so much of this tinned crap," he says suddenly, then gets up and heads to the kitchen. "Still got the makings for one decent dish. Just wait here, okay?"

Guess he really did need to talk. I could use someone to hear me out too. I'd like to be on the complaining end and get some commiserating myself. I hear so many stories around the disaster areas, but they're all other people's problems told to me. Tonight, however, is a little different. What can it be?

"Sorry for the wait. One order of stir-fried *fuki* and clams coming up!" A big steaming bowl comes this way. Beats cold out of the can any day.

"Looks great! How'd you rustle this up so fast?"

"Vacuum packs of clams. Relief contribution from some

thoughtful donor. Yesterday, when everyone moved to temp housing and we divvied up all the foodstuffs, I secretly set three packs aside. My privilege for being the cook at this relief shelter. I was up in the hills picking *fuki* when you came. Was thinking to eat them all myself, but here you brought sake and your company. Not an opportunity to pass up."

The stir-fry is delicious. The man can cook. "Great!" I say. Am I praising the chef or the flavor?

"Boiled the *fuki* to cut the bitter edge, then peeled and cooked them with the clams. Seasoned it with salt and sake and shoyu and pepper. The clams had plenty of flavor already. Would've been nice with red chili pepper too, if I had my druthers."

By now I'm quite drunk. Must have been tired from the long day—all the driving and visits from the morning on. The guy looks drunk too.

"But good news comes even at the worst of times," he picks up where he left off. "I was casting about in March, when one of my former clients asks me, would I like to join their branch office in Arizona? Seems they weren't doing so hot, since no one there was very clued in techwise. Must have been awfully bad for him to make me an offer like that."

"And did you accept?"

"Yeah. Sounded like a good thing to me. But I didn't want to do anything halfway, so I figured, as long as I was moving way over there, I might as well start with a clean slate and get rid of all my furniture and things. What little was left after the divorce. Anyway, I wasn't planning to take but two trunks. Simpler that way, or so I thought. I must have been feeling pretty desperate."

"Ambitious, you could say."

"Impulsive, you could say. Then I found there were things I just couldn't part with. Like my grandfather's glasses, probably from the early Taisho era, actually only the frames by now, but real stylish and they fold up in an ultracompact case. Not the kind that hook over the ears, these ride on the temples. The case was engraved with the name of a fancy optician in Sendai."

"A 'high-tone' gent, was he?"

"I never actually met him face-to-face. Then there was my grandma's Bible. All along the Kitakami River used to be Christian families here and there, and Grandma's was one of them. There was a photo of her pressed between the pages—brought back memories. She was a real beauty. Maybe she had a little Ainu blood in her, which is not so uncommon up here in Tohoku. Big eyes, well-defined features, very striking."

"Sounds like you idolized her."

"Close to it, I guess. Which made that Bible a real treasure. Or rather, the photo in it."

Do I have anything like that? I wonder. Nothing remotely similar. Kimura may say he's a sentimental old fool, but I envy him that.

"I also kept a bundle of old love letters. Just as a 'signpost on the road of life' sort of thing. I couldn't bring myself to toss them. But that's no reason to take them to America either. The only place I could think of leaving them was with my brother. We're not that close, but we're not on bad terms or out of touch either. So I call him up and explain the situation, ask if he could shove my stuff into a corner of his storeroom. I wrap everything up nice and neat to send by parcel post. I even ask when my sister-in-law is sure to be home so I can mark the delivery time on the label."

At this pronouncement Kimura glances up as if recalling something, indulging his emotions for one brief moment. The reverie, however, is painful: he looks like he's about to cry. Since then, everyone cries easily.

"The specified time I wrote down was on March eleventh, between two and four in the afternoon," is all he can say, looking down, then bringing the cup of sake to his lips.

I imagine the scene. Or rather the scene forces itself on me: a delivery truck cruising along. The driver might even have finished his deliveries when the quake strikes. Or else he's halfway to the brother's house and stops the truck to buzz the head office for instructions. He thinks the shaking has tapered off, so he continues his deliveries. Maybe he reaches the brother's house. Whatever, no matter where it was or when, somewhere the package he sent gets swallowed by tsunami waters. Carried out to sea, it becomes part of the ocean.

"When I heard about the tsunami and saw those impossible images over and over again on TV, I contacted my nephew in Tokyo. There was no getting through to my brother by phone. I just knew their house had to have been hit. I had to get up there right away."

He pauses, not for effect. More likely too many feelings crowd inside him.

"We left Tokyo in my nephew's car four days later. I figured there'd be no filling stations with gasoline anywhere en route, so we packed extra cans of gasoline and drove the long way around via Niigata in order to reach the area."

"Wasn't that even colder?"

"Blizzard conditions. Kept the heat on the whole time we were driving. When we finally did arrive, it was freezing. At first we slept in the car, then we stayed in shelters while combing the rubble every day and going around to all the collection points for dead bodies until finally I found my brother. My sister-in-law still hasn't been found. No special claims in that department . . ."

"But that's not to say . . ."

"No, that doesn't begin to say anything. . . . My brother and I weren't raised together, weren't especially close, but he was one of the very few kin I had. I didn't want him to breathe his last in a sudden crush of waves. I had to wait for days before we could get him cremated, but then the family plot was washed away, so we had no place to bury the remains. Eventually we were able to buy gasoline, so my nephew and I decided to take the ashes back to Tokyo. By then the Tokaido Expressway down the eastern seaboard had reopened, but it was still patchy and slow-going."

"Even now it's uneven, repairs all over the place."

"When I got back to Tokyo, I started getting ready for my move to America, but somehow my heart wasn't in it. It's like a voice was saying, 'You going to turn your back on all that you saw? That's your hometown even if you never spent a lot of time there. You didn't know anybody but your brother. The place was practically terra incognita. But still . . .'"

What would I do in his place? I don't have a brother or anyone else.

"No, really I did consider closing up shop and moving to America, though by the same token why not move to Matsubetsu? My livelihood would have been more or less guaranteed in Arizona, not to mention that American society is a lot more clear-cut than countrified Japanese ways. Keeping to the ready-made role of 'foreigner' would have been easy. That much I know."

So this is what he wanted to talk about.

"I'm thinking to make a go of it here, try living in the region as a local. I'm not saying I've got it in me to work the way my brother did, but I'll find something to do. Anyway, there's a drastic shortage of manpower here, I'll look into recovery or reclaiming or rebuilding or whatever they're calling it. Why not put the rest of my life to good use?"

His voice is firm. I wish I could celebrate his conviction, but it's not that simple for city folk to get by in the country.

"I had my doubts, but this vision kept haunting me. And it was sure to follow me to America, so I figured, no point in going there. I just knew I'd better go do what I had to do instead."

"What was that?"

"My grandma's Bible floating in the ocean. Swaying and sinking in the currents with her photograph still pressed inside. Or else lying motionless on the ocean floor, wedged between rocks, maybe, or layered among the rubble the tsunami carried out from land, or even resting under some corpse's head. It's gone for good, but if I stay here I figure I can always remember her face in the photo."

"I see." He got me. *I see.* How pathetic does that sound?

"So, well, I came to a kind of decision. I transferred my place of residence to my brother's old address. I didn't know whether you could change registration to a nonexistent address, but the mindless clerks in Tokyo processed it mechanically. No questions asked. When I got here I was a resident and asked to be admitted to the relief shelter. Been living here ever since. There's very few temp houses for single people, so I told them later is fine. What with my just moving here, can't expect special treatment."

Outside in the dark an owl is calling. Did the birds escape the tsunami unscathed? Maybe those birds nesting on the coast lost their young.

"It'll be tough building this town again from scratch. Wasn't very active to begin with, not much power, few young people, just political bosses putting on a show that the place was on the map. That's how things go, even at relief shelters."

I suppose, though each municipality is different.

"I know I'm not going to be calling the shots from here on, but it's still good that someone comes in from outside. A good twenty percent of the civil servants have died, after all. My guess is they'll put me to good use. There's a lot of uncertainties ahead, but Grandma's Bible is still somewhere here on the ocean floor."

I sink into a stupor, no balls to make any resolution of my own.

PIECES

Mitsuyo Kakuta

Translated by Wayne P. Lammers

"Your husband was with me that day," the woman across the table said. She looked even smugger than before, like someone bringing out her ace in the hole.

That's not the issue, Yuko stopped herself from snapping back. It really wasn't. But if she came out and said so, then the woman would feel as though she'd lost something more. Yuko understood how that worked. So she didn't say it. There was no reason to make the woman feel that way.

Instead she asked, "When's your birthday?"

This was the real question. She'd already been told the woman's age, but she couldn't help hoping it was a mistake.

The woman looked at Yuko as if she were speaking a foreign language. "April twentieth," she said, somewhat uncertainly.

"Of what year?" Yuko did her best to maintain a neutral tone.

Smugness tugged at the woman's face again, as if to say, *If that's what you're after, why didn't you just say so?*

"Nineteen eighty-three. I'm twenty-six."

So it was true. The woman—her husband's lover, who'd given her name as Mika Tokui—was unquestionably twenty-six years old.

So very young, thought Yuko, naturally enough, but that wasn't really the issue either. Yuko was quite openminded about such things. She saw nothing particularly strange or wrong about a sixty-six-year-old woman, say, taking up with a man thirty-eight years her junior.

Still, she did wonder, quite simply, what the attraction could be. What someone so young could have seen in her husband.

The only other customer in the dimly lit coffee shop was an office-worker type seated at the counter. Music played softly in the background—so low that it seemed to fall silent now and then. A narrow swatch of sunlight angled through the window by their table, lighting up a small triangle in one corner of the deep green tablecloth. Yuko absentmindedly traced the edges of the triangle with her finger.

The twenty-six-year-old Mika sat across from her saying nothing. Yuko wanted very much to see her expression, but she resisted the urge to look up. She kept her eyes fixed on the finger twining the sunshine and shade.

"Um."

Mika made a noise as if to speak, and Yuko raised her head. A tall, slender face, with a light complexion; large, well-defined eyes, slightly slanted; cheeks brightened with a touch of rouge; thin lips moistened with gloss. In some ways she looked like a little girl; in others like a grown woman. Yuko had never realized what an in-between age it was.

Her heart bore no enmity or hatred for the woman—nor even jealousy. Was it because she still couldn't quite believe it was true? Because she didn't believe Mika could really love her husband? Or was it because she'd already made up her mind?

"If I lose him, I have nothing left."

Yuko was taken aback. She'd expected Mika to sound a more defiant tone.

"You don't really mean that," she said without even thinking. "You're still young."

"No, it's true. There'll never be anyone else for me. I might meet somebody in my thirties, or maybe my forties— it's always possible. But no matter who it is, it won't be him. And if it's not him, everybody else is all the same."

I have nothing left. Suddenly Yuko found herself recalling, in strong colors, the time she had said those words herself. *It's really true. I have nothing left,* she'd said, just as this woman had done. On the verge of tears. Perhaps actually in tears.

She also remembered how badly it had hurt to be told, *You're still young.* It was infuriating. So what if she was young? Having her whole future ahead of her wasn't going to bring back what she'd lost.

"Are you going to stay with your husband even after knowing he was with another woman that night?" Mika asked. There was a quiver in her voice at the end, as if she was dreading the reply.

Yuko held her gaze. In the corner of her eye she saw the man at the counter get up to pay his bill. She decided to wait until he was gone before answering, and drew in a deep breath.

The wooden door opened and let in a band of sunlight, then swallowed up the brightness as it swung shut again.

"No, I'm leaving him. But it's not because he didn't come home that night."

She chose not to explain that it was because the two of them had reached a place from which there was no going back.

All expression seemed to have been plucked from Mika's face. Yuko could discern neither surprise nor joy there. No doubt she was turning the implications over in her mind. And it would come to her soon enough: If they're splitting up, then what am I worried about? We can go right back to the way we were.

Maybe so, thought Yuko. But she still felt no anger or jealousy. Not because she wasn't quite convinced about Mika and her husband, but because she knew. Even if they got back together, it would never really be the same for them. They would moan and groan about it, become frustrated and annoyed, feel let down and discouraged. But they could never again be the way they were. *It's true for me, it's true for my husband, and it's true for you.*

But that's not the same as saying you have nothing left. She offered Mika a word to the wise—though only in her heart.

"That day" was the day of the Great Tokyo Blackout. As usual, Yuko had been at the small editorial company where she worked. She and her colleagues were gathered around a computer in the conference room, selecting photos for a lifestyle magazine they produced under subcontract. It was to be a special issue featuring a certain trendy city, and shots of parks and bakeries and mom-and-pop stores, popular restaurants and bars, smiling couples and stylish young women filled the screen one after the other as comments flew back and forth: *This's a bit too far out there. That one's too old-towny.* Since the room had no windows to the outside, nobody noticed that the blue skies were filling with ominous clouds, and it wasn't until a thunderclap shook the room like an explosion that they realized a heavy storm had arrived. They emerged from the conference room to find torrents of rain being driven sideways against the windows and streaks of lightning crisscrossing the darkened sky like thin strands of thread.

"Better shut down!" somebody said, and hurried back into the conference room.

"Right," somebody else echoed. "Shut down in case we get a power surge."

People headed for their workstations or to check on things in the office kitchenette as the rip of thunder continued to split the sky.

They'd had a lot of this lately. As evening approached, the sky would suddenly grow overcast, and then a violent thunderstorm would roll in. Yuko had become used to it, and she assumed the rain would ease up again before it was time to go home.

A single gigantic flash filled the window and was followed almost instantly by a resounding crash, as if a wall had collapsed. Instinctively, she ducked her head and closed her eyes. When she opened them again, the room was dark.

"There went the power," somebody said. "Hope those pictures were backed up."

"Just in the nick of time," came the reply.

Yuko expected the lights to flicker back on more or less right away, but a half hour later they were still out. The darkness inside made the lightning seem all the brighter against the black clouds. Like strands of thread, like jagged lines, like a fireworks display, arcing bolts of electricity leaped across the sky and vanished. Surrounded by the relentless boom of thunder, she watched mesmerized, thinking how beautiful it was.

When the power had yet to be restored at four, the boss suggested they call it a day and go home. Lightning still flashed, but the thunder had moved off into the distance, and the rain was no longer coming down in buckets. They cleared out the freezer and pulled the plug on the refrigerator before all leaving the office together. At the station they discovered that the trains weren't running. Several people who lived relatively nearby said they would walk. The rest of the crew headed for the taxi stand.

Yuko went with the taxi group, but when they got there the line already snaked out of sight. Her home was only three stops down the line—a distance of no more than six or seven kilometers.

"I think I'll walk, too," she told her colleagues and set off on her trek.

Although the rain let up for good when she was about halfway there, every store she passed remained dark. It wasn't five yet, so the day had brightened again outside, but even so, she wasn't used to seeing convenience stores not lit up. It felt a little spooky, as if something terrible had happened.

She reached her neighborhood in about an hour. Even with the power out, the shopping street here was bustling with business as usual. Some places had fired up their backup generators to get the lights back on. Restaurants were operating by candlelight. In the gathering dusk, passersby floated dimly from one soft pool of light to the next. At the grocery store, keyed-up shoppers lingered in animated conversation. A power plant had taken a direct hit, one claimed to have heard. There was flooding all over downtown Tokyo, said another. Yuko listened to the chatter as she selected some ready-to-eat items for dinner.

She lived in a seventh-floor condo. Since the elevators were out of commission, she trudged up the stairs. After unlocking the door, she made her way down the hall by the glow of her cell phone screen to dig out a flashlight and some candles from the closet. As she moved from the kitchen counter to the dining table to the coffee table lighting candles, the room rose dimly out of the darkness in the soft flickering radius around each. Her thoughts finally turned to her husband. She tried to reach him on his cell but the call didn't connect. Wondering if the outage was affecting other parts of the city, too, she turned to the window and caught her breath.

Usually the view at this hour was a solid expanse of lights stretching as far as she could see, but tonight there was none. The entire city was wrapped in a pale darkness, like over the ocean at night. This must be something really serious, she thought, and quickly tapped out a text message. It failed to go through. She tried calling his office number with no better luck. Suddenly conscious of how stuffy the room was, she went to open the window, and fresh air poured inside.

She felt at her wits' end, but she didn't think her husband could have been struck by lightning or washed away in a flash flood, so she set about preparing dinner. Since the tap was dry, she had to make do with bottled water and wet wipes. The candlelight that bathed the table made it seem like a special occasion, and her heart quickened a beat. With some effort she uncorked a bottle of wine from her husband's collection and poured herself a glass, then sat down. A sea of blackness stretched outside the window. The moon hung directly overhead, but the urban ocean did not reflect its light. It's like traveling in a faraway city, she thought, sipping her wine and gazing at the unfamiliar view, no longer concerned about her husband.

She had almost finished eating when the landline rang. It was him. He wanted to know how she had fared, had she gotten home all right, and it brought her a twinge of guilt to be sitting there enjoying a relaxing glass of wine. He told her he was still at the office.

"Everybody's saying something really massive must've happened to the power grid. No trains or buses are moving. The rain here was coming down like you've never seen, and it turned Omotesando into a river. Were the trains there okay?"

If things didn't get moving again pretty soon, he said he would plan to spend the night at the office, so she shouldn't worry. She agreed that made better sense than going to great lengths to get home, and then asked if he'd be able to find something to eat—thinking even as she said it that it was a pointless thing to ask. He said he'd be fine.

As soon as she ended the call, she began to fret. What if the power stayed out all night? She had plenty of drinking water, but what about the toilet? What about charging her phone?

She sat back down in front of what was left of her meal and stared out at the lightless view.

It was utterly quiet. Normally, she would hear the faint clatter of train wheels in the distance no matter how quiet everything else became, but not tonight. The outline of Tokyo Tower on the horizon was of course lost in the darkness. When she lifted her eyes upward, the stars seemed brighter than usual. In spite of her unease, she was struck again by the beauty of what she saw.

The completeness of the silence made her feel as if she'd been cast out into a vast emptiness. Into a place as boundless as outer space.

Suddenly she was reminded of herself at twenty-six—of another time when she'd dined alone like this. That's right, she thought. She'd had this same sensation then. The sensation of being cast out, and drifting all by herself through some unknown realm that stretched forever.

She had discovered that she was pregnant. Since she'd been thinking she wanted to start a family soon, she was determined to have the baby. The question was the father, who was two years younger and whom she'd been dating for only six months. He stiffened noticeably when he heard the news, but he didn't say a word about her getting an abortion.

Instead, he said: "In that case . . . in that case, Yuko, let's get married. It's actually kind of cool that I'm already going to be a father, so soon after becoming a workingman." He grinned mischievously, as if making fun of his initial reaction.

With the baby due the following winter, they went to register their marriage at the beginning of summer. Then they visited each other's parents to let them know. The elders

fumed that they had the order of business backwards, and
Yuko's father, born in the first decade of Showa, was especially indignant. He absolutely would not recognize the marriage, he said, and refused to budge.

This came at a time when the economy was riding high,
and everybody believed the future held nothing but happiness. In the common perception, to be happy was to
acquire—to acquire money, to acquire position, to acquire
pleasures, to acquire a future. Accordingly, Yuko was happy.
She had garnered a husband and was expecting her first child,
which would give her the family she cherished; from there she
would no doubt go on to acquire a home, a car, in due course
another child, and continue straight on down the path to a
bright shining place.

The child was never born. Its heart quietly stopped beat-
ing inside her a short time after she and the baby's father got
married.

It was the first time Yuko truly experienced loss. She had
wept for days when her pet cat died, and again when her
grandmother passed, but the death of her own child was a
loss of a different order. What hurt the most, and what drove
her to despondence, was her inability to share the loss with
anyone. Her father seemed to have forgotten what caused him
to rail at her and offered his sympathy, and her new husband
consoled her with kindness. Her mother commiserated with
her by revealing that she, too, had suffered miscarriages—
two of them—something Yuko had never known. But it all
felt so distant. She was grateful for their comforting words,
but she also got the feeling that to them it was just someone
else's problem. After all, neither her father nor her husband
could possibly comprehend the physical pain that infused her

sadness, as if every last thing inside her was being gouged out of her. Perhaps her mother could—because she could remember her own pain. But it's not her loss, it's mine, thought Yuko. Since it was a loss that only she could understand, she had to bear it alone, and that was what made it so hard.

More than anything else, she detested being told that her whole future lay before her: *You're still young. You can have another baby anytime. Just relax. You have a long road ahead.*

Yes, she still had her future. She didn't deny that. It wasn't as if this had been her last chance. But she could think only of having to carry the burden of her loss for the entire duration of that future. She wasn't deliberately being perverse or trying to shut herself up in a shell. She simply could not stop thinking this.

It was the hottest part of the summer. Her husband had called to say he'd be late. Yuko prepared herself some dinner and sat down. There was beer in the fridge, so she poured herself a glass. She gazed out the window.

It's as if I've been cast out into the middle of nowhere, she thought. As if I'm adrift all alone in the darkest reaches of space.

She wanted to talk. Without voicing the words aloud, she tried speaking into the boundless darkness that seemed to surround her.

I'm pretty sure it was a girl. That's what the kiosk lady at the station told me. I bet your baby's a girl, she said. Because you have such a kind face. She said it right out of the blue one day, and it made me happy. Especially because my morning sickness was so bad then. She could be wrong, you know, my mother warned. You'd best stick with yellow for baby clothes. His mother, too. But I bought pink anyway. Even though I wasn't due for a long time yet. Does this mean I won't ever get to meet this child? Or could she come find me and plant herself in my belly again?

There was no one listening, and her words merely disappeared into the gloom, but it soothed her to talk. She felt as if she was finally getting a chance to share the loss that could not be shared. Strongly, positively, ever so closely.

Which apartment would that have been? She remembered putting their name in for a public housing unit but losing out in the lottery. It must have been the place they found after that in Mitaka—an apartment on the fourth floor of a five-story walkup. They couldn't see Tokyo Tower, but they could watch the town's annual fireworks display from their balcony.

Sitting at the table without her husband on the night of the Great Blackout, Yuko once again addressed the empty darkness with her inner voice, as she'd done when she was twenty-six.

I never did get pregnant again. I didn't see any rush. When I thought of the child who hadn't been born, it didn't seem right to try for another right away. But then even after that feeling had pretty much faded, I still couldn't get pregnant. We finally went in for tests to find out what the problem was. The doctor said there was nothing wrong with either of us, so he couldn't explain why I might not be conceiving. Eventually, somewhere in the middle of my thirties, I gave up. I accepted that my child wasn't coming back. I guess I was continuing to suffer the loss all that time.

The high times came to an end, and the economy kept getting worse and worse. The country entered a new century with no signs of recovery in sight. Whatever the rest of the world might think, Yuko now knew that to acquire was not to be happy. But she had yet to conclude that loss was not the root of unhappiness.

If happiness isn't to acquire, then could I be wrong to think unhappiness is to lose?

Suddenly, as Yuko was asking herself this question, the lights of the city burst to life as if in an ovation. *Click click click click, click click click click.* There was no actual sound, of course. The spectacle of millions of little lights turning on in such rapid succession brought her instinctively to her feet. Like a wave on the beach pursued by dancing white foam as it recedes, the line of light swept swiftly to the horizon, crawling floor by floor up skyscrapers in its path.

Glimpses of people she'd never seen before began spilling through her mind. Young lovers sharing a drink by candlelight. Children playing with some sparklers they'd just brought back from the store. The line of stranded workers waiting impatiently at the taxi stand. A middle-aged couple sitting across a table listening to the radio. A young camera buff taking pictures of the darkened city. A little girl stopping to gape at the stars twinkling like never before. A grandmother looking up at a ceiling lamp that had just come back on. . . . Like the sweeping wave of wakening lights, a dazzling jumble of fragments washed over her, sending her head spinning. Soon they gave way to glimpses of everyday minutiae. A battered old radio and a faded lampshade. A pile of dirty dishes and a rack of rippling laundry. A dwindling roll of toilet paper and the rasp of snoring. A darkened container of leftover stew in the refrigerator. A brown-and-black tiger cat walking across the yard. Each unremarkable fragment interlocked with the next like the pieces of a jigsaw puzzle. Their unexpected beauty made Yuko catch her breath. Then she was bewildered to realize that the fragments were not from the lives of strangers but from her own.

As she looked out over a city lit up again as if nothing had happened, it finally struck home. In the same way happiness could not be reduced to acquiring, neither could unhappiness be reduced to loss. Loss might sometimes bring unhappiness, but the two were not synonymous. For she had not been unhappy. She might never have had a child, but she still laughed at silly things, she still gazed at the view and wondered at its beauty, she still hummed catchy tunes when she was in a cheerful mood, she still gazed up at the clear blue sky and thought what a wonderful day it was, and she still had tender feelings for the husband who couldn't share her loss. Again and again and again. All these little pieces that made up her life had not been able to bury her loss; but neither had her loss been able to steal those pieces away from her.

The sensation she'd experienced all those years ago now came back to her. The sensation of sharing with someone the truth she had only then grasped. Strongly, positively, ever so closely, deeply, intensely.

Her husband came home on the first train the following morning. There didn't seem anything wrong with this, so she had no reason to question him. As they sat down to breakfast, she asked if he'd fared all right, and that was about it.

So it wasn't until later that she found out about the affair. When they went to a hot springs resort for their summer vacation, she saw him putting his cell phone in the drawstring bag the inn provided for carrying a towel and change of underwear when you went to the baths. It made her crack up.

"Nobody's going to call you about work here," she said, thinking he must be trying to inflate his ego by pretending he was indispensable.

His face drained of all expression for a brief second, and then he forced a smile. "It's just habit, you know," he said and laughed. But he did not remove the phone.

Oh, so it's for something besides work. When she'd seen the way his face froze, Yuko knew it instantly. Not merely suspected it; knew it.

But whatever this "something" was, she didn't think it needed to alter their relationship. In fact, it might be all the better if it ended without her ever knowing the details. If that didn't happen, then she'd want him to tell her, of course, but she had a hard time believing it wouldn't end. In any case, she made no effort to find out more about her husband's extracurricular activities while they were on vacation.

Then, a few days after their return, he suddenly volunteered a confession. It was the weekend, and they were having dinner.

"You know that day of the lightning storm—the day of the big blackout?" she said, intending to tell him how eerie the view had been from where she sat.

But before she knew it, her husband had turned deathly pale and was blurting out, "I'm sorry. I'm so, so sorry. I was with another woman that night."

Yuko sat with her mouth hanging open, at first not quite sure what she was hearing, then realizing that this was the "something besides work."

"But it's over," he quickly added. "I'm going to break it off. So I hope you can find it in your heart to forgive me."

Then why didn't he just end it and keep his trap shut? thought Yuko in exasperation. He was on unfamiliar ground,

It was hard to tell whether she was being sarcastic or envious.

"It's because I know I won't really lose a thing even if I walk away from twenty-six years of marriage," Yuko said with a grin.

Rather than smile back, Mika turned abruptly away.

Yuko dropped her eyes to the table. She saw that the triangle of sunshine had shifted, and her finger was now covered in shade.

SIXTEEN YEARS LATER,
IN THE SAME PLACE

Hideo Furukawa

Translated by Michael Emmerich

How do you convey what roof tiles are like to someone from a culture without roof tiles? Sure, you can give a dictionary explanation—say they're molded from clay, dried, fired in a kiln, and put on the roof of your house. They come in various shapes: slabs laid down in rows; half cylinders you use to cover the seams. You assume they must have originated in China and then made their way to Japan. One thousand, four hundred years ago, someone brought back roof tiles to Japan as a new "technique," and ever since they've been a standard element in the traditional Japanese house. In other words, they're just up there, on buildings. And now here they are in a pile on the ground at my feet. A miniature mountain at the edge of the garden, covered by a plastic sheet. Damn. Who'd have thought I'd ever find myself looking *down* at roof tiles? And outside the front door, a giant tile with a face on it, some sort of beast, specially fired—tiles like this are placed at the eaves as decorations. It looks like a sort of adorable dragon. Maybe if I said it's like a gargoyle in Gothic architecture, that would help people imagine what I'm talking about.

The beast looks like it's guarding the door to my parents' house, or maybe like it's looking for protection, for shelter, and our home is the shelter it's running to.

Our home. The house where I grew up. I haven't been back for ages—a whole year? I open the door, call in, Hello? I'm back! My wife: Hello! My mother and sister-in-law come out to welcome us, grinning. As I step up from the doorway into the vestibule, my eyes are drawn to an indentation in the floor, but it doesn't stop there. Two of the four walls in the entry are . . . how to put this . . . *gone.* Just *gone.* "What the . . . ?" I think, in a vocal sort of way. "Look at this, it's . . . this is awful," I'm saying. Posts exposed everywhere, beams overhead, half lost in shadows because they were never meant to be seen. My mother and my wife are talking now, exchanging greetings. "Isn't it?" my sister-in-law answers me. "And look at this, and this. And over here, too." There is a touch of excitement in her voice. This was the kind of thing you'd want to share, I could see that. Right after the quake, she says, the sky was visible through the roof. I realize with a shock that I can picture it. I knew the town authorities had declared the house "half destroyed," and my parents had told me over the phone about the fallen walls, but it had never occurred to me that it would look like *this,* that here in a still-habitable house there might be gaping holes, emptiness. Not just one wall, but two, *gone.*

"If the vestibule had collapsed they would've counted it as 'totally destroyed,' and then we would have been eligible for compensation," my sister-in-law says.

"Seriously?" is all I can manage. *Too bad.* Maybe that's what I ought to have said? My sister-in-law starts telling me about the neighbors' houses, the damage they suffered. She has a lot she wants to talk about.

So do my mother and my father. My father has problems with his legs, so I go in to talk with him in one of the Japanese-style rooms. He is really grinning, too. But hold on, what's this business about "one of the Japanese-style rooms"? If a house in Japan has Japanese-style tiles on the roof, it's obviously got to be "Japanese architecture," yet the vestibule with the two missing walls has an unmistakably Western feel, and in fact the house doesn't have all that many rooms with tatami floors. These are the Japanese-style rooms, and my father is in one of them. My wife and I kneel, talk with my father, mother, and sister-in-law, formally marking the fact of our return, our being together, and then my wife and I go over to the Buddhist altar. We light incense and pray before my grandmother's photograph. Next we stand and go over to pray at the small Shinto altar, clapping three times. Sometimes I get mixed up. You're not supposed to clap at a Buddhist altar, but as I'm remembering my grandmother, as my emotions get the better of me, I catch myself starting to clap. I realize now that it may be a little odd how we've made both Buddhism and Shinto part of our lives.

My father, my wife, and I each have a beer. It's between ten and eleven in the morning. My wife and I are staying until evening.

It is our wedding anniversary this day—this day in May 2011. Ordinarily we do something to celebrate the occasion, but the previous year I was away, on a fairly long trip to Mexico City, working on a project for a magazine, and so our fifteenth anniversary had passed without our marking it. This is our sixteenth anniversary. What to do? I suggested we spend a night in the hotel where we were married.

We live in Tokyo now, but we had the wedding in the town where I was born.

My hometown is about two hundred kilometers from Tokyo as the crow flies.

"Sounds good," my wife had said. We'd had this conversation toward the end of April. On May 15, TEPCO said it had determined that sixteen hours after the earthquake, Reactor 1 at the Fukushima Daiichi nuclear plant had a core meltdown. On May 24, the company said its data indicated that the cores of Reactors 2 and 3 had melted down, too. It had all happened months ago. And once a reactor core melts down, it doesn't melt back up.

So what are we supposed to do?

I spoke with my father over the phone late in March. My hometown is in Fukushima Prefecture, and it had experienced shocks that registered just under 6 on the Richter scale. The quake knocked over the gravestone where the names of our ancestors were carved, along with the vases and incense holders and all the rest. My father said he wanted to have the grave repaired. "Leave the dead alone for a while, they'll understand," I said. "First, the living should take care of the living." My family was going to need cash; any money they spent should go to the living. And yet . . . and yet. Our ancestors were buried in that graveyard—lots of them, there in that soil, in that town. People are cremated now, of course, so it's only their ashes that are buried, but until fairly recently our ancestors' bodies had gone into the ground there. And come to think of it . . . it wasn't like the dead could take shelter anywhere else. The graveyard *was* their shelter. Forever. Damn.

After we have a few beers, my wife and my mother and I take a walk around the property. My sister-in-law returns to her farmwork. The *kura* storehouse has been seriously damaged. There are greenhouses on the hill behind the house, glass and plastic; they don't look too bad. I feel relieved to see that. The small shrine to the family god is still standing. "That's what you think. It was in pieces, all over the ground!" my mother says. "Your brother rebuilt it." My brother is working, so we haven't seen him yet.

The family god. All the dead of the Furukawa "house" merged, became a single, collective ancestral deity. Wouldn't make much sense to people who think Buddhism is the only religion in Japan, I suppose.

From a Buddhist perspective, our ancestors are in the graveyard.

From a Shinto perspective, they're here behind the house, in the shrine.

But about my brother's work. And about the farmwork my sister-in-law is doing, and all those greenhouses we've just inspected. My father had started a shiitake farm, and now my brother has taken it over. Most of my childhood memories are of the woods, overgrown and dark, with lines of logs planted with shiitake spores. There were wild bamboo partridges, and I once saw a gorgeous pheasant. I'd watch squirrels bickering with crows in the trees, shudder at the sight of the giant slugs, enjoy the cruel game of plucking the thin legs off tall spiders. There was a canal, and a gloomy well.

Last year, my brother stopped growing shiitake on natural logs outside and switched to sawdust blocks that he plants with spores in the greenhouses. This decision turned out to have been fortuitous when, one day in April—April 2011, of course—shiitake grown in Fukushima using "open-air cultivation methods" (meaning logs in the woods) were banned in a dozen cities, towns, and villages after radioactive cesium was found in samples of the mushrooms. The fact that my family had escaped the ban put my mind at ease, at least for the time being—though at the same time, I felt bad for the other shiitake farmers.

Even if my family's business had been spared, the results of the sampling indicated that radioactive fallout was covering the woods. My own memories have been polluted.

My wife and I walk alone in another area with more greenhouses.

"Look, tomatoes!" my wife exclaims.

Later, my sister-in-law tells us they have started growing cherry tomatoes "as a test." It hurts a little to hear those words.

About a month earlier, my sister-in-law's father had died quite suddenly. Since we've been away so long, we obviously haven't had a chance to burn incense for him. So my sister-in-law, my wife, and I go to my sister-in-law's parents' house. It is still early in the afternoon. My sister-in-law has gotten to a stopping place in her work. By now I've consumed quite a few beers.

My sister-in-law's father's photograph stands on the altar. For the second time this day, my wife and I place our palms together to pray. I pray deeply.

Then we have tea. We talk with my sister-in-law's family.

"What'll you do with the paddies this year?" I ask.

"We're going ahead with them, same as always."

"You're going to plant them?"

"That's the plan."

"But what if they prohibit rice planting?" The soil was polluted by radioactive fallout, after all; there would be more inspections, rulings by the prefectural and national governments.

"Even if they do, we don't have any choice."

Sometimes my sister-in-law answers my questions, sometimes it's someone else from the family. Every so often my wife asks a question, too.

"Paddies go bad if you don't plant them."

"You have to till the soil, flood it, grow the rice."

"Otherwise the land goes bad?"

"That's right. It wouldn't be of any use for farming."

"It doesn't matter whether we can claim compensation from TEPCO later. Either way, we have to plant the paddies."

Even knowing they might never harvest the rice, or be able to sell it.

Wow. That hadn't occurred to me.

"The thing is, most of us around here, we like farming."

"Farming's hard, of course."

"Caring for living things, harvesting them—"

"It's not easy, but we like it."

"So no one's going to tell us to stop, to abandon our land."

Of course not, they agree. They sound bright, energetic. Strong. I hear the pride in their voices. My wife and I say good-bye; just outside the gate we stop and look at the field across the street. The owners are growing vegetables. A woman in farm-

ing clothes is tending to them. A white cat lies close by, licking
its stomach—the family pet, presumably. The cat seems to be
keeping an eye on the woman as it cleans itself. Afternoon sun
spills down over everything.

Damn, this place is beautiful.

My sister-in-law drives us back to the house—my family's
house. Finally I am able to see my brother. He's nine years
older than me. We open beers and say *kampai,* though my
brother has a bottle of sake waiting (1.8 liters) that he's
saved specially to welcome my wife and me. "Happy anniversary!" he says. My sister-in-law, my mother, and my
father join us around the table. It's covered with plates of
salted cucumbers, stewed vegetables, cherry tomatoes from
the garden, and bonito sashimi. We each have a single-
serving package of sushi from the grocery store, too. One
of the family's two cats wanders in and gets a few little
scraps of sashimi. I'd heard how panicked the cats were
on the day of the earthquake: one didn't come home until
the next morning, and then it just hid under the *kotatsu,*
trembling. The *kotatsu* was still in use on March 11, because
winter hadn't quite ended.

After that, there is a cake with "Happy 15th Anniversary!"
written on it in chocolate. The cake is a surprise. I realize
that during one of my calls I'd said we'd be coming back
because it was our fifteenth anniversary, so the mistake in the
number is my fault. Not that it matters. In the evening, my
nephew drops by. My brother and his wife's first son. Then
my sister comes by, too. She's six years older than me and
lives with her husband about ten kilometers away from here;

they have a strawberry farm. Their strawberries are very, very good. They have rice paddies, too.

"Is your husband going to plant the paddies?" I ask.

"I assume so," my sister replies. "He says he doesn't care what they say, he'll grow enough for us to eat. It won't kill us."

One resident of Fukushima Prefecture has committed suicide, driven to despair by what the fallout was doing to the crops—or rather by the damage being done by rumors even before the fallout could have an effect. That was in late March. That news hurt. Especially since the name of the area where my sister and her husband live was mentioned in the reports.

"Yeah, he was a friend of ours," my sister says.

I remember the mood then, in late March, when it seemed Fukushima might be abandoned, cut off as if it were no longer even part of Japan.

I'm pretty drunk by the time my sister-in-law drives us to the hotel. Our hotel. It is in town, and the feeling there is nothing like it is in the countryside where my family lives. I have all kinds of memories of the bustling area around the train station from my junior high and high school days, so even though I am tipsy I suggest that we go out for ramen. We wander the nighttime streets. A few drops of rain begin to fall. We don't have umbrellas. Whatever, who cares. It's a shock to see scars of the earthquake everywhere we look, even now, after all these months. An arcade that used to be home to the biggest bookstore in northeastern Japan has been taken over by seedy massage parlors and bars. That's a shock, too. Here and there we see posters that proclaim "Fukushima

Forever!" and "We Don't Give Up in Fukushima!" The cityscape shines, trembling, glistening in the rain.

We end up not having ramen, after all.

We go back to the hotel and immediately shower, first my wife, then me. Common sense. Because our exposure to the rain carries with it the danger of exposure to radioactivity. Then we sleep. Sixteen years since we were married. Sixteen years later, in the same place. Congratulations, dear. Congratulations to you, too.

Thank you.

The next morning, it's pouring. We check out of the hotel and get a taxi outside the lobby.

"Where are you from?" the driver asks.

"Tokyo," I say.

"Welcome to the Radioactive City."

Just then, I remember something. It could have come to me anytime, but it comes to me now. It's something I've read in the paper about an article in the British journal *Nature*: it could take anywhere from several dozen years to a century for Reactor 1 at the Fukushima Daiichi plant to be fully decommissioned. If it takes only thirty or forty years, I might still be alive when it happens. My wife, too. But if it takes a century? It strikes me, as I lean back in the cab, that I'm not going to be here then, and neither will my wife, nor the driver. No, it doesn't just strike me. I *understand*. None of us will be here then.

The wipers sweep the rain aside.

THE CROWS AND THE GIRL

Brother & Sister Nishioka

Translated by Alfred Birnbaum

鴉と少女

西岡兄妹

この見捨てられた土地では
太陽は本来の姿を取り戻し
その光のナイフでもって
諸物に色を刻んでいく

その内に
ひときわ黒い鴉の一群がある
止まった景色のなかで
唯一生命の躍動をみせる
ひとつの黒い有機体

Knife-sharp rays of a primeval sun carve colors
through the forsaken terrain.

A dark mass of crows descends, the sole sign of life
on this bleak scene.

And here, the corpse of a young girl.

そこには　一個の　幼い少女の　屍体

✿　✿　✿

内蔵はもうあらかたやられてしまった

片目はえぐられ

その甘露を鴉どもが奪い合う

Her eyes gouged out.

A sweet treat for crows to fight over.

Her innards torn asunder.

✿　✿　✿

彼女の身体は
その魂と共に
このおぞましい鳥の胃袋のなかに
散り散りになって収まっていく

しかしながらそれは
純粋に物理学的な
エネルギー保存の法則であり
彼らの営みを
おぞましいなどと
だれも責めることなどできぬ

Her body and soul alike dispersed into the birds' maws.

But that's purely the physical law of conservation of
energy; no one can accuse the scavengers of
horrid misdeeds.

✿　✿　✿

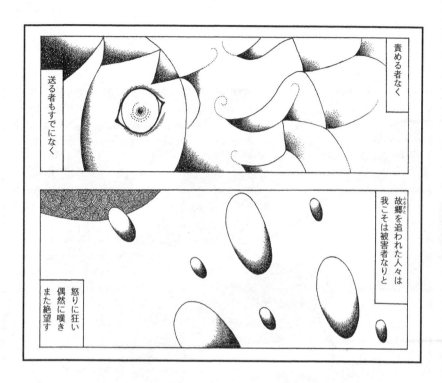

No one is to blame.

Nor anyone left to bid farewell.

People driven from their homeland may see
themselves as victims.

They fly into a rage, decry their arbitrary fate,
then fall into despair.

☆   ☆   ☆

だがこの一個の屍体をまえにして

彼らは正真正銘の加害者だ

And yet in view of this corpse,
they too are predators.

☆　☆　☆

民主主義というシステムの
後生大事に抱え込まれた
あるいはけたたましい無関心のための
あるいは金銭のための
アリバイのための
言い訳のための

その色々を背負わされてきた
あの民主主義というシステムの
これもまた
ひとつの答えなのだ

Their so-called democracy is just a system of excuses for profit, an alibi for apathy.

And this is the undoing of all that democratic scheming.

✿　✿　✿

Ignorance is sin.

Ignorance is evil.

✿   ✿   ✿

What is to be done?

What can be done?

✿   ✿   ✿

If anyone by now can still profess to believe,
blame God, blame Buddha, blame nature,
blame humanity.

✿ ✿ ✿

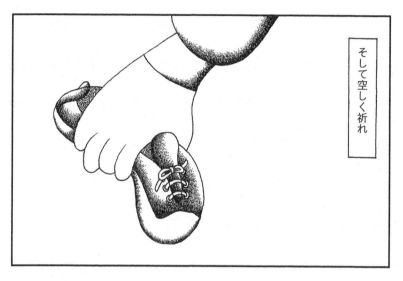

そして空しく祈れ

Then pray in vain.

✿　✿　✿

BOX STORY

Tetsuya Akikawa

Translated by Alfred Birnbaum

We'd been running short of boxes for quite some time. Families couldn't cope, they couldn't just wait around for a box to be delivered. Without boxes to put away toys and clothes, they couldn't clean up. Wastebaskets had disappeared, the streets were a mess. Everyone was late for school or work, trying not step in all the filth. The biggest problem was when someone wanted to give a present. Gifts went unwrapped, birthdays lost all their excitement.

Things looked bad. We all racked our brains for ways to get more boxes. The Legislature deliberated Box Supplementation Schemes for days on end, the ruling and opposition parties bickering over one basic issue: namely, in order to draft a bill for increasing production of boxes, they first needed to define what a box was.

Four sides and a bottom, maybe a lid, some stated the obvious, surely that was a box? But break those down, what do you have but cardboard and wood? Did not a box refer in essence to a hypothetical space, others quibbled, the empty volume partitioned off by those materials?

While legislators locked rhetoric, the box shortage grew ever more dire. Ultimately, despite no headway, the Box Supplementation Scheme was put into effect. It seems a noted university professor had invented a method for breeding boxes.

Every household was to breed boxes. That was the bare bones of the Scheme. Each day they were to talk to the little box delivered from City Hall, then leave it under a light for two hours each night. That alone would make it grow and, once it exceeded a certain size, give birth to baby boxes.

Very well, let us now consider the case of a woman who received one such breeding box. Miss Sato lived alone, having lost her parents early on. A hard-driven achiever, mornings she magnetically combed the riverbanks for iron sand for the Mining Cooperative; afternoons at the Hamster Electric Power Plant—or Hampo for short—she minded tens of thousands of hamsters. Thankless, backbreaking work. Each floor of the multilevel structure was scarcely bigger than the hamsters' treadmills, forcing humans to crawl on all fours to access the cages. Lying prone in that tight squeeze, she had to give the exhausted hamsters sunflower seeds and words of encouragement or, if she found an expired hamster, replace it with a new one. Every day Miss Sato dragged out dozens of hamster corpses, her heart aching with each one.

Given this heavy emotional burden, Miss Sato was none too keen about having to breed boxes. Some people were happy to gain a pet, because boxes that bore boxes definitely were some kind of life-form, and yet when those boxes grew too big, a collection crew from City Hall would come and cut them up. They'd become material to make new boxes, the staffer explained, but still Miss Sato had a bad feeling. Just thinking about where this all might lead gave her the creeps.

The box left by the staffer was light blue, twenty centimeters square, and, lift the lid, inside it was a brighter blue.

"Like the sky," murmured Miss Sato, admiring the pure hue. She flipped the flaps to steal a euphoric peek inside several times a day. None of the neighbors, it seemed, had received such beautiful boxes.

"Ours was gray," said Mr. Yone, her supervisor at Hampo.

"A box is a box, mustn't compare." She put on a gruff tone, intent on distancing herself from a rogue strain of doting parental pride.

"Once your baby boxes are born, City Hall will come collecting. Sorry, we mustn't get too attached."

But in actual fact, Miss Sato was quite taken with her light blue box. Just looking at it made her feel sky-high; she could almost picture clouds drifting inside. She was so glad they hadn't foisted a gray box on her.

Miss Sato put the box in the room next to her bedroom. As per City Hall's instructions, she talked to the box every day. She didn't mean to get friendly, but all too soon her words took on a familiar warmth. "What a nice box you are, a real beauty." "I bet when you get bigger all the other boxes will be jealous of how pretty you are." "Such a lovely box, what'll I ever store in you?" "Don't worry, I'm here. You can have your babies in peace."

The box never replied, but when she trained a light on

it at night, something rippled over the blue insides and top flaps—making it tremble slightly. And then the following morning, the box was definitely a little bigger.

In the two months since she began her duties, the box had doubled in size. Another month made it grow to some sixty centimeters square.

"I don't believe it!" shouted Miss Sato, cuddling the blue box. "You birthed!" Inside were three small newborn boxes, red and yellow and green, each the size of her palm. City Hall would collect these, of course, though breeding households apparently had the option of buying them cheaply. "So cute! So cute!" she repeated adoringly. Maybe she ought to buy one—but which?

The blue box kept slowly growing and giving birth to baby boxes, until the room was littered with baby boxes. Far more than was indicated in City Hall's breeding guidelines; this was one supremely fecund box. Miss Sato's cheerleading softened into kind appreciation. "You don't have to try so hard," she cooed, petting its top and sides, "you've already given birth to plenty."

Miss Sato carried the box into her bedroom, where she proceeded to confide all her problems. Why was she all alone in this world? And what about those poor hamsters fated to spend their entire lives spinning treadmills at the power plant? It pained her to see them each and every day. Moan and groan.

The box listened silently to all her complaints. Miss Sato felt much more at ease, as if untold toxins had leached from her being.

It was only after she'd talked out all her gripes that she noticed the box was rattling back and forth, flashes of light racing over the top and sides, enveloping it in wavelike patterns. A column of light shot up from under the lid and something exploded with a bang. Miss Sato cautiously lifted a flap to see—seven little newborn baby boxes in all different colors! At a loss for words, she gently rested her cheek on the box top and voiced an unspoken "well done" in her heart of hearts.

Actually, only a few days prior she'd received notification from City Hall to the effect that "First session boxes are to be collected shortly, together with all offspring boxes."

The very next day Miss Sato took off from both her magnet mining and Hampo jobs, and headed to the river with the nearly meter-square blue box in her arms. The time of parting was at hand. Resigned to the inevitable, Miss Sato thought that just once she'd take the box out for a picnic. She wanted to show the blue box the real blue of the sky.

A nice thought, but no fun. She just couldn't get in a happy mood. No, if anything she felt more and more like crying. But was she so sad simply because of the box's impending departure? Miss Sato couldn't tell. What was this box to her anyway? She hadn't even named it. Yes, but how grateful she was to her blue companion for listening to her words and relieving her of so much grief. In spite of which, they were going to cut it up. Wipe it from this world, make it cease to be.

"Say something!" Miss Sato pleaded with the box. Passersby strolling the embankment looked at the woman and the box. Verging on tears, yet aware of their stares, Miss Sato stood up, opened the box, and held it upside down with both hands. Suddenly the riverbank scene and all the windblown ways of the world seemed far, far away. Heedless of what anyone might think, Miss Sato pulled the box down over her and crouched to her knees.

The blue faded from inside the box, everything went black. Pitch black. And at last Miss Sato cried. She cried for her solitary existence and memories of when her parents were still alive. She cried thinking about all the hamsters who'd expired one after the next for the sake of humans and the fate of her box that was soon to be cut up.

Then, strangely enough, after what seemed like ages, when Miss Sato had cried herself dry, the Milky Way and distant stars twinkled into view, now fleeting farther and farther away. There was nothing anywhere around. She reached out, but her arms and legs touched no box. She was a lone speck, adrift in vast, dark space.

Yet even now as she strained her eyes, Miss Sato discerned the emptiness was filled with faint flickering entities. Presences longing to be born, she realized, precisely because there was a void. She couldn't make out what they were, baby boxes or embryonic stars, but that hardly mattered. Her own body now gone, Miss Sato slowly began to understand that in dematerializing she had become space itself looking on as beings came to birth from nothingness.

Everything existed within the box. That gut feeling was her last and ultimate awareness.

Citizens reported the abandoned blue box on the embankment, and a staffer came to collect it that very day. When they cut up the box, nobody noticed the single drop of water that dripped from inside. No one knew that in a far, far corner of the cosmos a galaxy had been born.

DREAM FROM A FISHERMAN'S BOAT

Barry Yourgrau

A man, perhaps you might call him a philosopher of an offhand informal type, rents a fisherman's little boat. He wants a break from the duress of the world, even though it's not yet summer (the traditional season of such maneuvers) but spring.

He goes drifting in the watery world somewhere south of Tokyo, off Kanagawa. In the boat's tiny stern, wrapped in his blanket, he sleeps snoring in the open, under the frosty stars. He wakes with the dawn. He smiles groggily. He toasts the sun rising from its floating pallet, and drinks. He refills his sake bowl, and toasts again, and sets to refill.

In his hazy drunkenness he feels a wave suddenly lift his little craft. Suddenly but gently, humpbacked, like a careful dolphin.

His sake bowl with its lotus decoration tumbles off its perch. The man blinks at it rolling about. A bad omen.

He swings around muzzily and gazes after the low, soft-shouldered wave as it pulses away shoreward, like a slight billow in a sheet. On the horizon beyond, the gleaming white wedge of Lotus Mountain pokes glistening into the cloudy sky of the new day.

In the boat the man rubs his unshaven chin, ominous-hearted. He thinks of a fearsome harbor wave: how, out in the open water, it seems nothing; a bump. Until it reaches the shore and explodes with the fury of a gorilla whale, in an orgy of terrifying destruction.

The man shivers. With a cowardly glimpse landward—a philosopher safely off in his floating world—he pulls his blanket around him and stumbles down the step into the boat's dark, cramped sleeping hatch. He sets his head on the rough pillow and draws his blanket up above his nose and seeks refuge from his foreboding in the maternal embrace of sleep, which here smells of fish.

His snores don't intimidate his fears.

In the man's dream, which gently rocks, side to side, the ghost of the poet of the ages is on the narrow road to the deep north. He wears a T-shirt with the silk-screened image of a spectral banana tree, an appealingly modest self-mockery of his name. The poet's ghost has paused in the neighborhood of Sendai, on the coast of Miyagi Prefecture. He is sitting in the mud. Beside him hunches a native son on Sendai, an actor known for his way with mayhem and destruction—but as a battler with honor and dignity, in a world devoid of these.

The actor is dressed in the style of his roles in famous yakuza chronicles, a lean, upright, fierce tough guy. Now "Shozo Hirono" (his name in scenarios) and the ghostly poet slump together shoulder to shoulder, weeping drunkenly amid the mud and devastation, sake bottles lying emptied beside them.

Through this gray landscape of disaster plod ghosts in puffy white outfits. But they aren't ghosts; they're hazard workers. They trudge among the muddy, gummy fissures and cracks that widen inexorably in the traumatized earth. Poisonous steam rises into the stunned air, like a toxic bonsai version of the eternal Milky Way. "I will be just as eternal," this little poisoned version boasts and threatens.

Here and there, a bizarre sight, vending machines lie on their muddied sides. Their inset speakers still dispense assurances to all, in voices broadcast from faraway by little craven cowards.

"*Everything is okay, all is fine and safe, nothing for anyone's concern,*" assure the disembodied voices from their broken vending machines.

The poet's ghost and the fake yakuza shake their drunken heads "no," cursing and blubbering.

The moans of the sleeper on his bobbing boat join in.

Then the dream on the boat whirls.

A giant wave thunders along, like a strange beast with a raging waterfall for a head and the twisting, coiling body of a serpent-dragon. On its tumultuous neck perches the grand old painter, feverishly dashing off sketches of the views of Lotus Mountain as they flash by—as the giant wave surges and writhes around Lotus Mountain, as if to knock it down, to pound it back into the island earth. Cars tumble past the old painter's flapping sleeve, shorn roofs and chimneys spin and tilt. Thirty-six, one hundred—a thousand glimpses of the besieged glistening white-capped pyramid the old painter is trying in frenzy to render. But his brush is long dry, his ink bowl long blown across him, his pages long scattered in the mayhem. He scratches and stabs his sketches on the withered flesh of his thigh with the wooden heel of his brush. The wave's howling froth tears at gray wisps on his old head, and he cackles, like a senile madman, silly and ridiculous—like an artist whose great art has been engulfed and overwhelmed. The giant wave's foam drenches him, slings itself on him like spittle from the foaming lips of a rabid giant.

Thundering along, the grand old painter suddenly flaps out a scrawny straining arm. His wrinkled face becomes a mask riven by anguish, as if constructed from the fissured and desolated landscape below. He flutters a withered hand in wild desperation at the besieged Lotus Mountain careening here, there, in his foam-blinded sight. His howls of grief are lost in the desolate thunder of the wave.

But they pierce the dreamer in his sleep.

He jolts awake, gasping in the boat's dark hatch.

"Lotus Mountain—" he blurts, his heart hammering.

Is it still there? He must go see, he must check, like a dutiful son. But he stays where he is, paralyzed. Or rather, inert. Lacking courage in his floating world.

He falls back again on his pillow, drawing the dim blanket around him, in his bobbing hideaway which smells of fish.

When his dream resumes, there is a small family sitting huddled on the cold, bare, muddy ground. They are a father, a mother, a young girl who is the daughter, and a younger boy who is the son. Under her weariness the girl has a bright charming intelligence, so you can imagine that in an animation movie fable by a great animation director—a poet of childhood, of its pains, its trials, its tribulations—the girl would play the plucky heroine. But now she just cries quiet, hopeless tears with the rest of her family as they prepare a meal. The meal is only rice. They have fashioned it into a small conical pyramid in their midst. In a way it resembles a child's model of Lotus Mountain. The water supply is not safe now, so they have boiled the rice in their tears.

With bare fingers they begin nourishing themselves, as best they can, scooping from the white pyramid of rice, eating the glistening grains.

This is the dream that a man has, who fancied himself a philosopher of life of a minor, easygoing sort, down in the hatch of a rented fisherman's boat, afloat on the world of a Japanese sea.

HIYORIYAMA

Kazumi Saeki

Translated by Jeffrey Hunter

Beppu was just coming out of the gymnasium.

Standing in the schoolyard, I raised my hand in greeting. He saw me immediately and came over.

Izawa had told me that Beppu and his family had lost their home in the tsunami, but were safe and staying at this elementary school turned into an evacuation center. When Izawa found Beppu here, he said, they hugged each other and wept; but Beppu and I were both composed now, maybe because of the presence of the reporter who had given me a ride to the center in his emergency vehicle. It was toward evening, and the smell of pork broth being cooked by Self-Defense Forces personnel floated in the air.

Quite different from his usual "smooth cool" look—he was a fan of Eikichi Yazawa and Tom Waits—Beppu was somberly dressed in jeans and a gray-and-black-checked work shirt. His hair, instead of being combed back and heavily pomaded, was lank and lusterless, and his chin had a salt-and-pepper stubble, but I was relieved to see him looking better than I'd expected. It was just a week since the catastrophe struck.

"They're all donations, these clothes," he said with a shrug, gesturing dismissively. Even so, I could see a red T-shirt peeking out from under the shirt. I smiled.

"I'm glad everyone in your family is safe," I said. "I was really worried when I heard your house had been hit. Izawa was volunteering with the meals, and he just happened to see your name on the list for this center. He's the one who let me know."

"Yeah. I guess he didn't think I was still alive, and when he saw me, he started bawling. I couldn't help myself, and I started, too."

As if to deflect attention from his slightly embarrassed admission, he urged me to come inside, acting as if he were inviting me into his own home.

I hesitated, not wanting to disturb the other evacuation center residents, but he just walked ahead, saying, "Come on, come on in," including the reporter in his invitation.

"But weren't you stepping outside for something?" I asked.

Using his index and middle finger, Beppu mimed smoking a cigarette.

We removed our shoes and carried them with us into the gymnasium. The floor was covered with blankets, and the large room packed with people. The reporter asked how many there were, and Beppu replied that there were about three hundred. The walls of the gymnasium, as well as those of the school building and the hallways, were plastered with notices about missing persons.

The gymnasium was chilly. With the supply-line cutoffs following the disaster, there was a shortage of heating oil. There were warnings on TV to beware of hypothermia, and here many of the elderly evacuees were tightly wrapped in blankets.

"This is my house now," Beppu said, indicating the boundaries of a space toward the front of the gym, in the middle of a row close to the stage.

Aisles in a checkerboard layout allowed us to reach his area. When I expressed my surprise at this, he said, "Yeah, it's funny, isn't it? Even in a place like this, people make these neat walkways, dividing the space into sections. See, I'm District One, Parcel Three. People have to mark off their space, you know," he explained with a wry smile.

Each person was allotted the space of one tatami. Since there were six in Beppu's family, they had an area of about six tatami covered with blankets. I recognized his youngest son, an elementary school student, lying on his side and playing a Pokémon card game, but the rest of the family was elsewhere.

"Please, come on in," Beppu said, with more than a touch of irony.

We sat down on a camel-colored blanket in one corner.

"Now, where's that tea? Or would you prefer coffee?" asked Beppu, crouching in front of us.

"There's no need for that kind of thing at a time like this," I said, shaking my head and waving my hand emphatically in protest.

"Don't be silly. You took the trouble to come visit me. I can't send you off without at least a cup of tea," he said with humorously theatrical exaggeration. He exited his "house" and headed toward the stage. There were several benches, with cardboard boxes of food supplies and thermoses of hot water.

As I sipped the half mug of instant coffee he had given me, I noticed a copy of *Selections of Tang Poetry* on the blanket. Beppu enjoyed literature, and he had run a cram school for elementary and junior high school students in his house. I taught a writing course after I moved back from the city to my hometown here fifteen years ago. I had been supporting myself doing double duty as an electrician and a writer, but I came down with asbestos poisoning. Beppu was one of my students, and we became occasional drinking buddies. Izawa was another of my students.

"I thought it might bring me a little peace of mind. I had a friend bring it to me," Beppu said.

"So 'The realm is in ruins, but the hills and rivers remain'?" I asked, delivering the only line from a Dufu poem I knew by heart. I sighed and thought, no, the realm is in ruins—*and so are the hills and rivers.* I had just come from visiting, with the reporter, the little harbor town where Beppu's house once stood. The Self-Defense Forces and police were still looking for the dead, and only emergency vehicles were allowed entrance.

Beppu nodded silently.

The reporter, his single-lens reflex camera hanging from his neck, began to walk around the evacuation center.

It seems a miracle that I'm even here now. Sometimes I wonder why. I wake up in the morning, right? I think, am I dead? No, I'm alive.

But somehow, you know, I still don't feel alive. It's like . . . it's like I'm just pretending to be alive. . . .

I was alone at home when the earthquake hit. The kids were at school, and my wife was at the community center, at a thank-you party for the teacher of our oldest daughter. She graduated from junior high this spring.

Anyway, it was the strongest earthquake I've ever felt. The Miyagi Prefecture offshore earthquake a few years earlier was a hiccup compared with it. The shaking was incredible, and it just went on and on. To be honest, I thought the house was going to come down around me.

When the shaking finally stopped, I tried to clean up a little. The dressers and bookshelves had all toppled over, the kitchen cupboard doors had flown open and all the plates and dishes were on the floor, in pieces. A complete mess. I was trying to put things in order when the giant aftershocks began, one after another, but I wanted to get the broken china and glass swept up before the kids came home.

Then the sushi chef from the restaurant next door came and said I needed to get out of there. Why would I want to do that, I asked, and he said that there might be a tsunami and I should go to an evacuation center, just in case. Yeah sure, I said, just like last year. You remember, Shigezaki-san, I was going to go drinking with you that Sunday at the end of February last year, but then there was the earthquake in Chile and I canceled at the last minute because they were saying we should head to the evacuation center in case there was a tsunami? It's going to be the same again, I thought—sitting for hours in the evacuation center in the community center, and then nothing happens, and you end up going home again. I wanted to get the house cleaned up, so I said no, I was staying.

My wife had taken the car, anyway, and I had no way to get there. And there hadn't been any tsunami warning. Now of course I know that with no electricity they couldn't sound it.

But the sushi chef said he'd drive me in his car, and he was very insistent. That's when I remembered that my wife had called me before the earthquake to say that she'd left her cell phone at home, and she asked me to drop it off for her when I had a moment. There was nothing at all strange or different about the sea at that time. We started driving to the evacuation center, but along the way there was a big traffic jam. Nobody was moving, so I said let's get out and walk. Just then I happened to look back the way we'd come, and I saw, at the far end of the road, the straight horizontal line of an incredibly huge, tall, black wave coming toward us. At first I thought, no, it can't be—a tsunami. Now I was really worried. I told the chef to just leave the car where it was, and we started running for our lives, toward a junior high school that was another designated emergency evacuation center. It was a little farther from the tsunami than the one we were going to.

Just as I was about to pass through the school gateway, I tripped over something and hit the dirt. The tsunami was right behind me, and it was a very close call.

At that point Beppu, who had been talking in a jovial tone, as if sharing a funny story, laughed.

Although I worried it was inappropriate, I laughed too. "You played soccer in high school," I said. "You must be a good runner."

"Not anymore. This was more than five hundred meters. My heart was pounding, and my legs felt like they were going to fall off. . . . You know, you probably think that a tsunami comes down on you from above, don't you?"

I nodded, recalling a scene from a surfing film, where the crest of a wave, looking like a shark's mouth full of sharp teeth, was engulfing a person from above.

"That's not what happens. It comes right after you while you're running away from it, licking your heels, then pulls the ground beneath your feet away. You get knocked off balance, you fall backwards, then the next surge gets you."

Beppu suddenly fell silent, as if actually remembering the scene he was describing.

When I awoke on March 13, two days after the earthquake, which measured magnitude 9.0, I stood, as I always do after I get up, by the living room window and looked out to sea. After a moment, I rubbed my eyes and looked again.

I've lived on the ground floor of this apartment building, which sits on top of a hill about one hundred meters high, for thirteen years. This morning something was different.

The red-and-white-banded chimney of the waste incinerator plant stood, as always, a little to the left of the apartment building. The fact that no smoke had risen from it since the earthquake, when normally it burned every day except during the New Year's holiday, was not what I noticed. What I noticed, when my eyes finally focused, was that the forest along the coast had only one . . . two . . . just a handful of pines. It looked like a scene of the African savanna that you see in television programs or photographs.

I had never paid much attention to it before, but that stretch of land used to be filled with green rows of thickly planted pines that had hugged the sandy shore, and the sea glittering beyond them. Now the line of pines looked like a comb with most of its teeth broken. I guess that's how it is, I thought; you don't notice things until they're gone.

The sea loomed, and because the pines were gone, it seemed bigger, somehow. On both sides of the river separating us from the next town were several ponds that hadn't been there before, dully reflecting the sunlight.

That area used to be . . . houses! It came to me in a flash. Those ponds used to be houses!

The electricity had been off since the earthquake, so we didn't have TV, and the only news reports we could get were from an emergency radio that you had to crank to charge. Since the quake we'd been completely occupied putting the house back in order and going for water, since the water and sewer were out. There hadn't been time to gaze out the window.

A chill ran down my spine. I had heard on the radio that the coastal areas had been hit by the tsunami and hundreds were killed, but it hadn't really sunk in. Now I was seeing incontrovertible evidence that the horror had actually happened. I hurried to the bedroom to wake my wife.

Electricity was restored three days later. We watched the images that played over and over on TV, and I realized that if I had seen this immediately after the disaster, the scenes of people and cars and houses being swallowed and swept away by the wall of water, I wouldn't have been able to bear it.

Then came the scenes of explosions at the nuclear plants in neighboring Fukushima Prefecture. In front of our window, we could see Self-Defense Forces helicopters constantly flying back and forth, fire and rescue sirens wailed nonstop. We were filled with anxiety.

"Look. You can see real good from here," said Beppu to his daughter, pointing toward the sea. "See the big bridge right in front of the ocean? It's to the right of that."

"Oh, there. Oh. There's nothing there," his daughter, wearing her junior high school uniform, murmured.

Five days after we had met in the evacuation center, Beppu called to say that he was going to check the posted exam results for his eldest daughter. She had taken the entrance exam for the high school at the foot of the hill where our apartment stood, and he wondered if he might stop by.

Of course, I replied, and less than ten minutes later he arrived in a car driven by one of his friends. I asked how his daughter had done, but without answering, Beppu walked toward the living room window. From behind, he looked equally as if he could be making a proud display of a happy result or trying to compose himself before announcing bad news.

We were still experiencing powerful aftershocks, so we'd laid our stereo speakers and floor lamps flat on the floor. The electricity was back, but we remained without water or gas, so fifteen plastic bottles of drinking water and two twenty-liter polyethylene containers of water for cooking were also lined up on the floor. There were also two cardboard boxes of emergency rations—rice, dried bread, canned foods. These were the emergency rations that we'd put together prior to the earthquake, having been told there was a ninety-nine percent chance of a major earthquake hitting the area within three decades.

We boiled water on a propane-cylinder burner on the table.

"Beppu, enough suspense! How did she do?" my wife demanded, pouring the tea as we sat around the little *kotatsu*. Six years younger than me, she's the same age as Beppu and is considerably less formal with him.

"You tell them," Beppu said to his daughter.

Blushing and smiling, she made a little V sign with her fingers—almost out of sight, below the edge of the table.

"Well, that's wonderful!" said my wife happily.

"She was the only one in her class to pass the exam for this school," added Beppu, more than a touch of pride in his voice.

"That's just great . . ." I said, stumbling. "I'm sorry, I'm afraid I've forgotten your name."

"Nozomi. With the kanji for 'hope' and 'ocean.' "

"Right, Nozomi. You came up with that name, didn't you, Beppu?"

Beppu thrust out his chin, pleased. He'd brought Nozomi to our house on several occasions, and she seemed to be his favorite.

"Just a minute," said my wife, as if remembering something, and she went to the kitchen, returning in a moment with some milk tea and pound cake.

"Let's celebrate," she said, smiling. "It's a cake a friend in Tokyo sent us in the emergency."

Nozomi softly brushed aside her bangs as she ate.

"Here, you can have mine, too," said Beppu, handing her his plate.

✲

I spent the night the tsunami hit with Nozomi.

When I reached the junior high school serving as an emergency evacuation center, it was full of evacuees, and the front stairs to the second floor were crowded with elderly people in wheelchairs from a retirement home. I couldn't get up that way, and just about then water started rushing into the entryway. I looked around, remembering an emergency stairwell in a corner and ran toward it. I may have been saved because this was my old school, and I knew it so well.

I got to the second floor, but the water kept rising, so I went up to the third floor, and finally to the stairway landing that led to the roof. I spent the night on the landing. It was cold, and snow was falling lightly. The windows were broken, everyone was wet, and we were all shivering. When the water retreated a bit, I gathered up classroom curtains and uniforms from the soccer club and handed them out to people, to help fight off the cold. Then, at some point, I noticed my daughter was with me.

Our three kids in elementary school spent the night at their school, my wife stayed at the community center, and my daughter and I were at the junior high. I was worried about the others. I sat in a daze, unable to speak, just staring at the floor in the dark. Then in the middle of the night Nozomi said, "Look, Dad, the stars are so pretty." Who cares about the stars at a time like this, I thought, but I looked up and saw the sky filled with stars. Everything around us was dark, and the stars were the only illumination. The earth had been transformed into a hellish realm, but the stars still sparkled, unchanged. . . .

✧

"They really were beautiful."

My wife and I nodded.

I'll never forget the beauty of the stars that night, when all the electricity in the town was off. There was a quarter moon, too.

One afternoon a little more than a month after the quake, Beppu came by with a car. Some sake made three days before the disaster had been miraculously discovered amid the rubble of the sake brewery, which had been swept out to sea by the tsunami.

"The chief brewer is one of my students. He came all the way to the evacuation center to let me know," Beppu explained. And as alcohol wasn't allowed at the evacuation center, he asked me to join him for a drink. The buttons on his blue shirt were open to reveal a flashy T-shirt with a likeness of Kiyoshiro Imawano, Japan's "King of Rock."

"Where did you get the car?" I asked.

"An old high school friend whose company transferred him to Tokyo this spring lent it to me while he's away."

Beppu was the kind of guy who had a lot of friends and an in with everyone.

His own car, which had been carried away by the tsunami, was a compact, but this was a seven-passenger station wagon, and he had a hard time maneuvering it on the winding road down the hill from my house. Along the way there were fallen cement-block walls and collapsed shoulders. The old inn that once stood on the opposite side had been completely destroyed, and one lane was blocked off to traffic.

"Did you feel that big aftershock the other day?" asked

Beppu when we got onto the highway. Although the road appeared flat at first, the quakes had caused numerous gaps in the pavement, which was wildly uneven, and the car jolted violently.

"Yeah, it was a big one," I replied, grabbing on to the handle above the window to steady myself. "I don't know, it really . . . got to me somehow."

Thinking that the aftershocks had pretty much subsided, we'd gotten the furniture and bookshelves back in place and put things away. Then we had another quake, intensity 6, magnitude 7.4, almost a replay of March 11. It was deeply disturbing, as if the rug had been pulled out from under us all over again.

Many of the buildings that had somehow survived the first quake were half or completely destroyed by the new one. The earth beneath our apartment building had sunk fifteen centimeters in the first quake. The second one dropped it another ten centimeters, exposing the water pipes and creating large fissures between the foundation and the ground, where rats had taken up residence. The only positive thing was that there wasn't another tsunami.

"It was the middle of the night, too. Whenever there's an aftershock, the backboard of the basketball hoop at the evacuation center rattles."

"Oh, yeah, the one that folds up into the ceiling," I said.

Well, it just happens to be right over where my family sleeps.

Whenever it starts rattling, I hug the kids to keep them from being afraid. It must have happened dozens of times already.

But that night, it wasn't rattling, it was banging and shaking so much I was afraid it might fall down on us at any minute. To make things worse, the electricity was out, so it was pitch-black. I half stood up, covering the kids with my body in case the thing fell. Men were shouting, "It's a big one!" and women were screaming.

Then suddenly the generator kicked in and the lights went on—right over my head.

Everyone had their little heaters going that night and the gym was steaming hot, so I was sleeping in my underwear. So there I was, in my underwear, in the spotlight! I'm going to be ribbed about that for a long time.

"Wow, this area is a total mess. Looks like it's been completely untouched since the quake."

"Yeah, you're right."

On the way to get the sake, we drove through the residential area across the river from where Beppu's house had been. It was the same stretch of shore that I had looked at from the living room window, where all the pine trees had been washed away.

I knew a lot of people who had lived here. Someone told me about a woman who watched as her husband got carried away by the tsunami before her very eyes, as he was trying to put the car in the parking lot of the evacuation center. That first day I visited Beppu at the evacuation center, I drove through here with the reporter, and today, a month later, it was still pretty much the same, although the water had receded a bit.

Flattened cars were scattered across a vast, salt-caked tidal swamp. Any cars that still retained their shape were either marked with a white X—meaning that the emergency crews had searched them and found that they were either empty or their occupants were safe—or a red X, meaning that the occupants were dead. I saw a decorative gold spoon on the ground; pine trees torn up by the roots; adult videos; a dictionary of agronomy; framed photographs of family members, generations back; a box of onions that had sprouted long green shoots; cushions; bedding; a chair in the middle of an open field, as if someone had been sitting there until a moment ago.

Daily life had been swept away.

"Not a great year for flower viewing, is it?" said Beppu, looking down at blossoms on a branch of a cherry tree that had been mowed down along with the pines.

All right, we're here. That's where the sushi restaurant used to be, and this was my house. You remember going to his place with me, don't you, Shigezaki-san? Must have been about thirteen years ago, I guess. There was a little boy who wanted us to play toy trains with him, remember? The chef's son. He's a university student now. Last year he entered the mathematics department of a national university, which means he's smart. The sushi chef is insisting that he's going to reopen his restaurant here, but I wonder. The city is saying they aren't going to permit rebuilding near the shore.

Me? Well, my wife and kids are saying that they don't want to come back here to live. To be honest, I don't know what I'll do.

It's all gone, isn't it, except for the foundation. This was the entryway, and my classroom was there, right after you entered. The blackboard was here, and the students' desks were here. The house was in the back, and my room was on the second floor.

All that survived was this one big platter for serving sashimi. It's strange to say this, but it's also kind of a relief to have it all gone like this. I'd been feeling a little stuck lately, like I was at a dead end, going nowhere.

Surprised by that statement, I looked into Beppu's eyes. But I couldn't discern his real feelings.

"Want to go to Hiyoriyama?" he asked suddenly.

About two hundred meters farther back from the sea was a small man-made hill. The houses that had once surrounded it were all gone, but the hill had withstood the tsunami.

Beppu coughed several times as we walked toward it.

Right after the tsunami, everything was wet from the seawater, and there were few asbestos or other particles in the air, but now things had dried out, and the air felt heavy with asbestos dust. Bulldozers were rumbling around noisily, pushing the debris into piles. The cleanup effort was moving forward at a quick pace, and in a little more than a month, a great deal of the debris had been cleared away, creating an expanding vacant space. We called it debris, but these were the things that surrounded us, the objects that supported and sustained our lives; no matter how many times I witnessed it, it was hard to bear watching it all treated as garbage.

"You know, I never dream about things before the earthquake. Only what happened after. It's not that I have nightmares about the tsunami or anything like, but . . ."

"Now that you mention it, it's the same with me," I said.

"Really? You, too? I don't . . . it's like everything around me is changing so much, and I have no control over it. I find it hard to think clearly. I wish I could at least somehow stop time from slipping away along with everything else," said Beppu softly.

At Hiyoriyama, we found one big pine tree still standing in the middle of the back of the hill. The cherry trees and the little shrine, about a meter square, that had stood on the hilltop were gone, but the pine remained stubbornly anchored in place.

"Someone who witnessed the tsunami, and survived to tell it, said that the wave washed right over the top of this tree."

The pine was about ten meters tall.

Thirteen years before, I had climbed this hill with Beppu when I was writing an article for a magazine. According to the information I'd gathered at the time, there are more than eighty places in Japan called Hiyoriyama—"Weather Watching Hill." They're near harbors to the open sea, and none of them is taller than a hundred meters. In the old days, there were specialists, experienced weather watchers, who used to ascend the hill, observe the movement of the clouds and the wind direction, and predict the weather. They probably also watched the tides and the flight of birds. And they also were the first to see signs of an approaching tsunami after an earthquake.

I recalled that there was a stone memorial with an inscription about tsunami at the foot of the path and looked around for it.

It was still there, toppled sideways, on the other side of the hill. Beppu and I read the inscription on the large,

2.5-meter-tall stone aloud, working out the antiquated syntax together.

MONUMENT TO THE EARTHQUAKE AND TSUNAMI: BEWARE OF TSUNAMI FOLLOWING EARTHQUAKES

A powerful earthquake was suddenly felt at 2:30 a.m. on March 3, 1933, followed forty minutes later by a giant wave accompanied by a mighty roar. The wall of water was ten feet tall, forcing its way up the Natori River and flooding the area from Enko in the west to Teizanbori and Hiroura Inlet in the south. More than twenty homes were inundated and several thirty-ton-class motorized fishing boats moored on the banks of the Natori River were washed ashore into farmers' fields at Yanagihara. Though many smaller boats were destroyed, fortunately there was no loss of human or animal life. The damage was much greater in the inland counties of Mono, Oshika, and Motoyoshi, as well as Iwate and Aomori prefectures, due to the fact that the earthquake's point of origin was in the ocean approximately one hundred fifty leagues east-northeast of Mount Kinka and the full force of the tsunami was blocked by the Oshika Peninsula, so that only smaller waves reached the shore here. . . .

When we reached the part "fortunately there was no loss of human or animal life," Beppu commented bitterly, "It's all happened before, you see. And they made this monument, even though no one was killed."

Standing atop this man-made Hiyoriyama, just six meters in height, we had an unforgivingly open, 360-degree view.

The last time I was here, the hill was surrounded by homes, and you couldn't see the ocean. Now I was confronted with a vista of dunes stretching into the endless distance and white waves washing up against the shoreline. To the south, I couldn't see as far as the nuclear power facilities in the neighboring prefecture, but the chimneys of the geothermal power-generating facilities were visible; and to the north I could see the petrochemical complex of the industrial port and the peninsula behind it. One reason may have been because all the coastal trees had been washed away.

Beppu motioned me to look behind us, and in the distance we saw the three television towers rising from the hill where my apartment building stood. We used to watch the fireworks they set off down here every summer. It suddenly occurred to me that in a way I also lived on a Weather Watching Hill.

At the top of Hiyoriyama were handmade memorials to the victims of the disaster, with words and messages written on scraps and slats of wood painted white. An elderly woman, her hands clasped together, was praying.

"Let's go to where the sake brewery used to be. Izawa has volunteered to wash the bottles, so he'll probably be there, too."

As we made our way back to the car, Beppu told this story:

"Wataru overheard some of us adults at the evacuation center talking about 'this world' and 'the other world.' Know what he said?"

"Wataru—he's your youngest?" I asked, remembering the boy playing with his Pokémon cards.

"Yes. He said, 'So, Dad, what world are we in?' He doesn't talk about it, but he must have seen a lot of people being washed away."

What world is this, I asked myself, between this one and the other?

RIDE ON TIME

Kazushige Abe

Translated by Michael Emmerich

Another day of uninspiring waves. Nothing bracing about the wind, either—it just feels chilly. Occasionally a regulation gust springs up, as if it suddenly realized it should have been blowing all along, flapping the banners outside shops before moving on, leaving in its wake the salty sting of the rocks and sand swirling.

The waves are always the same. It was like this yesterday, and it'll be this way tomorrow, too. Bland, ordinary swells, unremarkable, average.

Still, we know they're not as bad as we say they are.

Truth is, we've gotten used to them. Used to their excitements.

Having spent so many years on this coast, paddling out past the breakers day in and day out, all year long, we've become familiar with the way the wind blows, the way the waves break, the lack of surprises—unless something really out of the ordinary comes along.

Lucky enough to be served gourmet meals on a daily basis, we grumble about the cooks above the clouds. *This isn't good enough, do better!* Grousing about the weather bureau has gotten so old, we don't bother.

We're like passive chicks in a nest, necks straining upward, mouths open, cheeping every so often, waiting for food.

We're bored, but that doesn't stop us. Because we have a reason to be here. Because we can't give up hoping that someday a wave of legendary proportions will come crashing toward this shore again.

Some of us still can't believe it was real.

A monstrous swell that appeared a decade ago, so huge it staggers the imagination, the likes of which has never been seen again.

That's what we've been yearning for all this time, that's the wave we've been dreaming of—a dragon flapping its wings, so huge it blots out the sky.

The rookies are only half-persuaded that it ever really existed. But the veterans know. Whatever, we all want to come face-to-face with a legend.

That's who we are. The surfers who make this northern shore our home, passing our days in unrelieved monotony.

We've forgotten who we were, but sometimes, rarely, we see what we've become.

Of course, just because a place is beautiful, you don't necessarily want to stay forever. You lose your edge. You fall prey to routine, you get worn down.

Matted hair, grainy with salt; faded raglan T-shirts; white

jeans dyed muddy; mirrored Polaroid sunglasses—that was our look. True, some of us were wearing prescription sunglasses, but it's not like any of us were old or decrepit. And so what if we didn't look so great.

Now, after all this time, we look like skeletons. Even the kids have skin so dry it's like sandpaper; they're popping vitamins just like the rest of us.

Years of surfing have turned us into a bunch of moaners, complaining that none of the waves are any good, but that's just an act, it doesn't mean we've lost our enthusiasm.

Just the opposite, in fact. We complain, it's the predictable situation we're used to, but we still want the thrill of a ride. We like to think we've got the patterns of the waves figured, even though no two are ever the same. It's just talk, our boredom, but we're not going to change. And so we go on talking cocky—things will be the same tomorrow, and the next day.

Our goal hasn't changed: to be here when the groundswell comes.

But if we were honest, we'd have to admit we've been so coddled by the smooth, easy waves on this beach that none of us is really ready to take on such a monster.

And now here we were, headed for a Friday unlike any other.

There was a tweet. At last, it said, this is the one you've been waiting for.

It was almost, like, a certainty. The wave would hit the shore on Friday.

This time, it seemed the information could be trusted.

This legendary wave was approaching, for the first time in ten years, and the best surfers were preparing. That's what they said anyway. The new faces, the younger surfers, not believing it was actually going to happen, must have been scrambling to gather all the information they could. Those who'd wiped out the last time and wanted a second chance were waxing their boards like crazy, hardly noticing their hands were numb.

And yet, with a wave like the one we were expecting, there were no veterans, no rookies. Because nothing you read in a manual, no regular technique, would be of any use.

Forecasters said it was almost 100 percent certain the wave would come on Friday.

The date got a double circle on smartphone surfing apps, and figures in the Fishing Co-op all said Friday was the day. An old surfing judge who was the best at predicting waves, not one easily fooled by talk, said he had no doubt it was the leviathan.

Everyone was psyched.

Last time, every single surfer had wiped out.

Me included. Truth is, I was barely able to stand up before I slammed into the massive wall. Nobody could ride that wave.

This time, though, we knew better.

Whenever new surfers arrived, they heard from the locals right off how people had died trying to ride that monster.

Each time the dragon wakes, always in early spring, it swallows a few of us, then vanishes again for years.

The same terrible scene has played out over and over. And each time, the locals tell the newcomers all they've witnessed, and make them listen.

The sharper the account, the better the listener.

The better the listener, the less meaningless death is.

Because when those memories are passed on, they point the way, and make it less likely that so many will go down the next time.

A decade ago, we were knocked off our boards, it's true, but everyone made it back to shore. Because we had learned something from the past.

The experiences of the old surfers, handed down from one generation to the next, were leading us closer to matching the force of that huge wave.

Manuals and techniques were a start, but history was the key: history was the teacher.

And so we had to try again. Try, once again, to come out on top.

A decade of calm waters had turned us into tough-talking wimps, but even people like us could be useful, lending our history to try to accomplish some sort of breakthrough.

The wave was coming. It would hit the shore on Friday.

On Friday, we would put on our wetsuits just like always, head for the shore at the same hour we did every day.

The only differences would be the class of the wave and our determination.

But this was going to be a mega-grand swell fifty meters tall, and the worst could happen.

So I guess the truth was, everything would be different.

We needed to be in our best form, to be ready for a Friday unlike any other.

Who knew, if we were physically in peak condition, and if we could keep calm, maybe we could turn a Friday unlike any other into a Friday just like every other.

Three hundred people, including surfers and spectators, stand on this beach.

We're all staring at a legend that has become real.

We knew what to expect, more or less, but the awe-inspiring

force of this ten-year wave stuns us: surfers, forecasters, and the surfing judge, all gaping.

Everyone is transfixed, no one says a word—it's like being at a movie, overwhelmed not only by the quantity of water but also by the thunderous, even majestic roar of the wave, filling in our silence.

I'm wondering whether this might be as far as we get, if we will just stand here, unmoving, to the end, watching the monstrous wave, when I hear a voice.

One surfer breaks from the group and dashes into the surf. Another follows, then a third. They're paddling toward the wave.

The dragon responds by revealing more and more of itself, spreading its wings to strike at these pathetic humans.

The surfers try to ride and slide from the crest into a superlong ride. They all go down.

That doesn't stop other surfers from running into the sea, boards in hand, slapping them down into the water.

It's about time, I suppose, for me to paddle out, try to get to the top of the wave.

I may fail again, but at least with three hundred people watching how I go down, something of use may come bobbing up somewhere, somehow.

And whatever that is, it will bring us one step closer to the breakthrough we're all waiting for.

Maybe then we can make a Friday unlike any other just like every other.

I know we can do it. Here I go.

LITTLE EUCALYPTUS LEAVES

Ryu Murakami

Translated by Ralph McCarthy

In late summer 2011, Typhoon No. 12 hit Japan, causing disastrous flooding and landslides in the Kansai and Chugoku regions and even affecting, in a small way, my home in Yokohama. The winds were nothing compared with what harder-hit areas experienced but strong enough to topple the eucalyptus I had planted in our garden two years ago. The young tree, which had grown about four meters tall, was snapped just above the roots, and in its fall crushed our plum and olive trees, even reaching our cable TV antenna on the fence.

I'm not one to putter in the garden, but I had to do something about the tree stretched out across the yard. I had no tools, however, so I went to the local home-and-garden center. The store had a variety of chain saws on display. They made me think of Jason in *Friday the 13th,* and they looked like they'd be perfect for dismembering trees, but since I could think of no other use for such a thing, I decided it'd be wasteful to buy one. I ended up purchasing a regular pruning saw and an axe.

I started by whacking off the smaller branches with the axe and used the saw on the larger ones, and eventually I reduced the tree to a limbless trunk about thirty centimeters in diameter. I sawed what was left into logs about fifty centimeters long, split them, and stacked them on the terrace. Eucalyptus trees grow fast, so the wood was soft and easy to saw through, and very fragrant, too. Known for its powerful antiseptic qualities, the eucalyptus was apparently known as the "Australian fever tree" in recognition of its role in preventing the spread of malaria.

Bundling the leafy branches together proved more strenuous and time-consuming. Gathering the branches, pruning them to about the same length, and tying them into bundles took nearly two hours. The thought occurred to me, as I was sweating from expending all this energy, how minuscule this was compared with something like, say, the cleanup after 3/11. This was just one tree. Cleanup after 3/11 was beyond inconceivable.

About two months before the fall of my eucalyptus, I had traveled to Miyagi Prefecture to do research for a television program I host. Four months had passed since 3/11, but rubble and debris of every imaginable sort still littered the landscape. Along the coast of Sendai, a city whose finances are on relatively solid ground, a gigantic disposal and recycling site had been set up and construction had begun on a large incineration facility. At the disposal site, the refuse was separated by category—concrete, metal, plastic, vehicles, appliances, lumber, scrap wood, dirt, textiles, and on and on. They were in enormous piles that called to mind the pyramids of Egypt. It was surreal. The hot midsummer sun beat down, millions of flies buzzed about, and a repugnant odor hung in the air. I began to feel that I had no business seeing this. It was a strange sort of déjà vu—I had felt similarly upon first viewing photographs of Auschwitz. I remembered one of a warehouse in which the possessions of gas chamber victims—shoes, clothing, jewelry, eyeglasses, even locks of hair—had been sorted into various piles.

I left Sendai for Okumatsushima, where a number of villages still lay in ruins. The devastation seemed endless: a fishing boat split in two, grounded on someone's porch; cars and trucks half buried in the mounds of mud outside flattened houses; scraps of lumber and chunks of concrete entangled in the felled remains of trees. And everywhere you looked were little red flags with names written on them, marking spots where victims' bodies had been discovered. These flags were reminders that the debris wasn't mere wreckage that needed to be cleared away but rather materials, equipment, and tools that had supported and sustained people's lives.

After removing the horizontal eucalyptus from our garden, I went back to my real job. I had research to do for the novel I'm working on. The book I was reading, *Uejini shita eireitachi* (The Heroes Who Died of Starvation), by Akira Fujiwara, claimed that the majority of Japanese troops who died during the war in the Pacific died not in battle but of starvation, malnutrition, and disease. The Imperial Japanese Army had not only ignored logistics but gave little consideration to geography and climate as it continued to send troops to the Solomon Islands, New Guinea, Burma, the Philippines, and other battle zones. The result was a staggering number of collateral deaths.

In May 1942, hoping to capture strategically important Port Moresby on the southern coast of New Guinea, the Imperial Army decided to blaze a trail overland from Buna on the northern coast. The 17th Army's South Seas Task Force, stationed at the front, expressed the opinion that an overland attack was not feasible. Between Buna and Port Moresby were 360 kilometers of dense tropical jungle, and bisecting the island was the Owen Stanley Range, with mountains as high as 4,000 meters. There were no roads, meaning that sheer manpower was required to keep the troops supplied with food. Under the prevailing conditions, the most a man could carry was 25 kilograms of the main staple, rice, and considering the topography and climate, he couldn't have traveled on foot more than about twenty kilometers a day. If you subtract the amount of rice that the bearer himself would consume, in order to support a force of 5,000 troops, each requiring 600 grams of rice per day, the army would need 32,000 men—more than six times the fighting force itself. In other words, a land attack was a practical impossibility. But the planners of the war judged the opinion of the frontline task force, which actually knew the local conditions, to be "overly pessimistic" and ignored it. The attack on Port Moresby was launched, and within a month, food supplies ran out. The troops ended up not battling the enemy, but having to battle starvation.

Why was such a reckless and irrational strategy implemented? The principal reasons would appear to be the Imperial Army's disdain for logistics and local intelligence; their fanatical idealism; their disregard for the human rights of their own troops; and the inflexible, pyramid-style chain of command. Some of these characteristics of the old army remain, unreformed, in many Japanese organizations today, although it can't be denied that a lot of progress has been made.

Immediately following 3/11, more than 10,000 members of the Self-Defense Forces participated in rescue operations in the disaster area. The entire SDF consists of some 24,000 troops. What with logistical support, rotation of personnel, information gathering, and communications, one wonders if virtually every person in the SDF wasn't involved. Forces mobilized from the Ground SDF alone included the Northeastern Army's 6th and 9th Divisions; the Northern Army's 2nd Division, 5th and 11th Brigades, 7th DHQ, and 1st Artillery Brigade; the Eastern Army's 1st Division, 12th Brigade, 1st Engineer Brigade, and Logistic Support Group; the Middle Army's 3rd and 10th Divisions, 13th and 14th Brigades, and 4th Engineer Brigade; and the Western Army's 4th and 8th Divisions and 15th Brigade; not to mention its Central Readiness Force, 1st Airborne Brigade, 1st Helicopter Brigade, Central Nuclear Biological Chemical Weapons Defense Unit, and NBC Counter Medical Unit. In the four days following the earthquake and tsunami, these forces rescued some 19,000 people.

If the SDF had retained the worst characteristics of the old Imperial Army, lifelines of various sorts would have remained severed in the disaster area. It's unlikely that an organization like that could have rescued 19,000 in four days.

✳

Ten years ago I wrote a novel in which a middle school student delivers a speech before the National Diet. "This country has everything," he declares. "You can find whatever you want here. The only thing you can't find is hope." I mentioned this in an article I wrote shortly after the initial disaster, which concluded as follows:

"Today evacuation centers where supply lines have broken down are facing serious shortages of everything, including food, water, and medicines. We have had shortages of goods and power in the Tokyo area as well. Everyone's lifestyle is threatened, and the government and utility companies have not responded adequately. Yet, for all we've lost, there's one thing we have regained. The great earthquake and tsunami have robbed us of resources, civic services, and many lives, but we who were so intoxicated with our own prosperity have once again planted the seed of hope."

Whether that hope has taken root and sprouted, these several months after 3/11, is not a certainty. Hope is like faith. It's a notion or feeling that things will be better in the future, and it becomes necessary when misfortune makes it difficult to go on living. We see quintessential examples of that in refugee camps around the world and in nations and regions ravaged by war and civil strife. People who find themselves in a scorched postwar wasteland bereft of their homes, their wealth, their families, need to look for hope somewhere.

After 3/11, the word *hope* popped up everywhere in Japan. The recommendations submitted by the Reconstruction Design Council in Response to the Great East Japan Earthquake, convened by the prime minister, Naoto Kan, carried the subtitle "Hope Beyond the Disaster." Japan has been inundated with the word, but I'm not so sure that the populace is filled with the conviction that a better future is coming.

I've come to feel, however, that hope isn't something that permeates the whole. Hope isn't born all at once, like buds erupting in spring; nor does it envelop the landscape like freshly fallen snow.

After the eucalyptus tree was disposed of, I dried some of the wood shavings in the sun and then put them into a wineglass on my desk. Before beginning work, I drop some eucalyptus essential oil on this homemade potpourri, and a refreshing, invigorating fragrance fills my study. I've never had any interest in aromatherapy and such, but I was seduced by the scent that hung in the air when I was sawing through that tree.

I also saved about ten twigs to use as cuttings. After a bit of research on the Web, I soaked the ends in water for a day and a night, planted them in small clay pots, and lined them up on top of my bookshelf. It'll be a couple of months before I know if my cuttings will take root and grow. But it makes me feel good to see the "baby" leaves on the ends of the cuttings waver in the breeze from the window.

I think that maybe hope is like one of those little eucalyptus leaves. You suddenly become aware of its existence and potential; you figure out what you need to do, and you set goals; you gather information and knowledge and, if necessary, capital; and then you take action. Whatever the scale of the project, the buds of hope at first seem tiny—insignificant and unreliable. There's no way to be sure that they'll really blossom. But once you make the first step forward, possibilities begin to take shape and show themselves.

Katsunobu Sakurai, the mayor of the city of Minamisoma, which was devastated in the earthquake and tsunami and contaminated with radiation as a result of the Fukushima Daiichi nuclear disaster, had this to say about recovery and reconstruction:

"If we bring in general contractors from Tokyo, whose recovery are we talking about? We'll do the work here ourselves. The Ministry of the Environment permits burial of waste with readings of up to 8,000 becquerels. The tsunami breakwater was destroyed, and the coastal region is flooded each time there's a typhoon or big waves or a particularly high tide. The important thing here is to rebuild the infrastructure. We'll construct a bigger breakwater and bury the waste with acceptable radiation levels behind it. What we call debris was once the stuff of people's lives. We're working on a plan for a protective shoreline forest to be planted on top of the reclaimed land. And we're looking a hundred years, two hundred years down the road. We need to go about this calmly and steadily" (*Aera*, 8/8/2011).

Buds of hope are definitely popping out, one by one.

AFTER THE DISASTER,
BEFORE THE DISASTER

David Peace

*In an emergency such as this earthquake, art is use-
less, to say the least. Our recent experience only helped
expose the ultimate futility of all artistic endeavours.*
—Ruminations on the Earthquake,
Kikuchi Kan, 1923

A fter the disaster, Ryūnosuke lived for four more years.
Before the disaster, Ryūnosuke had been in his study
in his home in Tabata, in the north of Tokyo. Throughout
the morning, there had been brief showers and a strong wind
while Ryūnosuke read newspaper reports on the formation
of a new cabinet under Count Yamamoto. Just before noon,
he had finished the last article and lit a cigarette when he felt

a slight vibration. Moments later, his house was shaking to an extraordinary degree and Ryūnosuke could hear tiles falling from the roof above him and his family screaming from other rooms below him. But the shaking did not subside, as was usual, and the motion continued to intensify. Ryūnosuke put out his cigarette. He tried to stand but the floor tilted and rolled again beneath his feet, so he was forced to sit back down at his desk. Then, at last, the waves of shocks seemed to lessen and Ryūnosuke could finally stand and join his family outside in the garden.

His wife, his children, and his aunt all rushed to Ryūnosuke and clung so desperately to him that he feared he would fall over as, monotonously, he repeated, "It's okay. It's okay," while thinking, *It's not okay. It's not okay.* For still now, in the garden, the ground continued to rumble, continued to sway, heaving and tossing, the air filled with the fog of a smothering dust and the screams of grinding timbers.

After the disaster, the official record would state that the Great Kantō Earthquake had started at 11:58 a.m. on Saturday, September 1, 1923, and stopped after four minutes.

After those four minutes had passed, his wife and his aunt immediately began to bring essential provisions and the family's most valued possessions out of the house. They lined them up in the garden. His wife suggested Ryūnosuke do the same with his most treasured books. Ryūnosuke went back inside to his study. Many things had fallen or moved since he had last sat at his desk. He righted piles of books. He straightened sheets of paper. Then for some time Ryūnosuke stared around the room at his collection of books, wondering which to save and which to forsake: Baudelaire or Strindberg? Flaubert or Dostoyevsky? But Ryūnosuke did not want to read poetry. He did not want to read drama. He did not want to read short stories or novels. Ryūnosuke picked up a volume by Voltaire. He put it back down. He picked up a volume by Rousseau. He put it back down. Finally he picked up the Bible and *The Communist Manifesto.* Ryūnosuke took them out to the garden. He pulled a leaf off a *bashō* plant. He put the leaf on the dirt of the ground. Then he put the two books on the green of the leaf. His wife and his aunt both looked at him with contempt. Ryūnosuke could not tell if their disdain was directed at his choice of books or at his treatment of the plant. Or maybe it was not contempt. Maybe it was fear—

"Look! Look! Look," shouted his eldest son, Hiroshi, pointing at the sky.

From the gate of their house on the hill, Ryūnosuke and his family saw thick black clouds of smoke rising from the fires that now were raging across the lower parts of the city. Ryūnosuke and his family knew they had been spared the worst of the quake and, so far, the ravages of the flames. A few loose tiles had slid off their roof and smashed on the ground. A stone lantern near the gate had toppled over and broken into pieces. Ryūnosuke gathered up the fragments of the tiles. He stacked them neatly in a pile. But then the ground shook again and the pile collapsed. Ryūnosuke stared at the fragments of the roof tiles and then at the four pieces of the stone lantern. He tried to right the base of the lantern but it was too heavy to lift. He left the fragments and the pieces lying where they had fallen.

That afternoon, first his half brother and his family arrived, then his sister and her family. Both his half brother and his sister had lost their homes in the fires following the earthquake.

Both their families were now homeless. Ryūnosuke, as first-born son and head of the family, now opened up his home to his half brother, his sister, and their families. Later that long afternoon, they were joined by the son of one of his wife's relatives from Honjo, on the eastern bank of the Sumida River; he had been standing with a shutter over his head, to ward off the sparks from the flames, when he was picked up by a whirlwind caused by the fires and then dropped in the pond of the Yasuda garden. He was the only one of his family of nine to survive. Before moving to Tabata, Ryūnosuke and his family had also lived in Honjo. *Had we not moved*, thought Ryūnosuke, *then surely we would all be dead now, too.*

And again the earth shook, again a strong aftershock, and again tiles fell from the roof of the house, as again his family rushed to Ryūnosuke, hanging anxiously on to him, his half brother, his sister, and their families, too. And so tightly did they all hold on to his *yukata* that Ryūnosuke feared he would be strangled in their clutches.

That evening, the head of the Neighborhood Association called on Ryūnosuke and his family. The head of the neighborhood association asked Ryūnosuke if he and his family were all healthy and well, their house habitable and safe. Then the head of the neighborhood association told Ryūnosuke that martial law had been proclaimed, that all troops in Tokyo had been mobilized, and that anyone refusing to comply with requisition orders would be subject to three years' imprisonment or a 3,000-yen fine. Now the head of the neighborhood association asked Ryūnosuke if he, as a Good Citizen, would join their newly formed local Committee of Vigilance, so he, as a Good Citizen, could help safeguard their neighborhood during this period of uncertainty and upheaval. Ryūnosuke, as a Good Citizen, nodded. Now the head of the neighborhood association handed Ryūnosuke a helmet. And Ryūnosuke, as a Good Citizen, put it on.

That night, no one dared to sleep indoors. The ground continued to shake, shattering people's nerves, while the very air itself seemed to choke them, so hot were the temperatures. And more visitors continued to come—to check on their welfare; to borrow their money, eat their food, and drink their water; to share their reports of destruction and fire— *Honjo-ku, all burned; Hongō-ku, all burned; Shitaya-ku, all burned; Kōjimachi-ku, the Palace and the block south of Hibiya Park safe; the Imperial Hotel and the district south, safe; Koishikawa-ku, the river Edo side burned; Kyōbashi-ku, all burned; Shiba-ku, mostly burned; Azabu-ku, partly burned; Ushigome-ku, safe; Yotsuya-ku, mostly safe; Asakusa-ku, all burned; Nihonbashi-ku, all burned; Akasaka-ku, the half toward the city center burned; Fukagawa-ku, all burned*—and share, too, their rumors of insurrection and invasion, their accusations of arson and looting, their whispers of murder and rape, their words of death and fear.

Under the stars, beside his helmet, Ryūnosuke lay on the futon between his wife and two sons. He tried to read the Bible. But he could not concentrate. He tried to read *The Communist Manifesto*. But, again, he could not concentrate. For under the ground, he could feel the earth continue to grind and scream, a gigantic mechanical worm burrowing through caverns and tunnels, pushing the ground up, then pulling it back down in its wake. Ryūnosuke imagined the turning gears and spinning cogwheels deep within the metallic body of the beast. And above the ground, he could hear their visitors continue to accuse and whisper. Ryūnosuke put his fingers in his ears, his fingers in his eyes, and waited for the dawn.

✻

After the disaster, that first morning, Ryūnosuke was over-come with worry for his friend Yasunari. Yasunari lived in Asakusa and, throughout the long night, all the rumors and whispers Ryūnosuke had heard had filled him with dread for the fate of his friend; he saw the delicate, refined face of Yasunari broken and crushed beneath the weight of a build-ing, pale and bloodless, or his thin, hollow frame burned and charred on a mountain of corpses, black and anonymous. And so with a great sense of foreboding and some degree of duplicity, for fear of worrying his wife and family, Ryū nosuke set off for the Asakusa area.

The journey from Tabata was not an easy one for there were no streetcars and the roads were clogged with survivors, children strapped to their backs, shouldering enormous bun-dles or pushing handcarts piled high with their belongings, all heading out of Tokyo, in the opposite direction to Ryūnosuke. A military law had already been passed that allowed people to leave Tokyo but forbade others from entering, and so there were soldiers and police on every corner. There were Com-mittees of Vigilance, too, formed by Good and Upright Citi-zens, all carrying clubs or pipes, sticks or swords, and often wearing helmets similar to the one Ryūnosuke now sported. As he walked toward Asakusa, Ryūnosuke watched as these committees dragged men from the columns of survivors to accuse them of being non-Japanese, either in blood or spirit, and up to no good. Without fail, these accusations were punctuated by blows from the clubs or pipes, sticks or swords of the Committees of Vigilance. Ryūnosuke was certain that had he not been wearing his new helmet then he, too, would have been subjected to such accusations and blows. Or worse.

Finally Ryūnosuke reached Asakusa. Or the place where

Asakusa once had stood. For here the destruction was total; mile after mile of completely burned and still-smoking ruin, from the river in the east in every direction, and everywhere corpses; charred-black corpses, half-burned corpses, corpses sprawling in gutters, corpses floating in rivers, corpses piled up on bridges, corpses blocking off whole streets at intersections. Every manner of death possible to a human being was on display. And everywhere, the stench of death; an odor of rotting apricots that, even through the handkerchief Ryūnosuke pressed against his face, burned his nose and scalded his eyes with horror and grief. For now, finally, tears came as he remembered the people and the place Asakusa once had been—the little pleasure stalls, all now cinders, the pots of morning glories, all now withered—

All now harrowed. All now dead.

And Ryūnosuke despaired for Yasunari. But then, at that very moment, he heard the very voice of his friend and Ryūnosuke turned; he blinked; he blinked again; he rubbed his eyes with his handkerchief and blinked again. But yes! Yes! It was true! Here, among all this destruction, among all this death, here was Yasunari, alive and unhurt, walking toward him across the rubble, through the smoke, in animated conversation with Kon, another of their friends.

"I thought you were a ghost. I was sure you were dead," said Ryūnosuke.

Yasunari laughed. "Everyone is a ghost now. A ghost or an orphan."

Yasunari and Kon were walking up to the Yoshiwara to see what had become of the old pleasure quarter, and they urged Ryūnosuke to join them. And as they picked their way through the wasteland, Yasunari never stopped jotting down words in his notebook or recounting his recent adventures and observations—

"In the moments after the first great shock, before the fire consumed my lodgings, I was able to salvage some bedding. And so, last night, I slept on that in the park. I even managed to construct a mosquito net. And then, who should crawl under the net beside me, but my landlord's wife and her child. . . ."

But when the three friends came upon the Yoshiwara quarter, even Yasunari fell silent in the face of what they saw there.

The Benten Pond was now a cauldron of five hundred corpses, bodies piled upon bodies, some burned and some boiled. Muddy red cloth was strewn up and down the banks, for most of the dead were courtesans. Ryūnosuke stood among the smoldering incense, his handkerchief pressed to his face, his eyes fixed upon the corpse of a child of twelve or thirteen years. Now Ryūnosuke looked up at the sky, his eyes smarting with the smoke and the sun. He wanted to cry out, to scream at the gods:

Why? Why? Why was this child ever born, to die like this?

And again, as he had many times before, Ryūnosuke saw the image of Christ on the Cross and again he heard the words that haunted him:

My God, my God, why hast thou forsaken me?

Beside Ryūnosuke stood a young boy of a similar age to the corpse. The boy was staring at the body. He stifled a sob. He looked away. But his older brother grabbed his arm, gripped his face, and scolded him. "Look carefully, Akira. If you shut your eyes to a frightening sight, you end up being frightened forever. But if you look everything straight on, then there is nothing to be afraid of."

Suddenly, Ryūnosuke felt the eyes of the young boy upon him. Ryūnosuke turned to smile at the child. But when their eyes met, the boy hid his face in the folds of his older brother's clothes. Ryūnosuke turned on his heels and marched off. Ryūnosuke thought, *It would have been better had we all died.*

✶

After the disaster, on the way back to Tabata, under a tangle of scorched electric lines, Ryūnosuke fell in step with a policeman. As the two men walked, Ryūnosuke questioned the policeman at length about the earthquake, about the fires, and about the various rumors of crimes and insurrection that seemed still to fall from every passing mouth, hanging in the air with the stench of rotting apricots.

The policeman, perhaps impressed by Ryūnosuke's helmet, was talkative but confessed that while he knew many had been accused of malicious or revolutionary acts, he himself had seen no evidence of such deeds.

Just outside Nippori Station, Ryūnosuke and the policeman came across the body of a man tied to a pole, his head beaten in, his body horribly mutilated, with a sign around his neck that declared he was both a Korean and an arsonist. The man must have died by inches and even now, perhaps hours after his slow death, as Ryūnosuke and the policeman stood before him, another passerby approached to whack his corpse with a rolled-up parasol. This passerby now turned to Ryūnosuke and the policeman; he thanked them for their good work, bowed, and then sauntered off, swinging his now-bloody parasol as he went. The policeman shook his head. He urged Ryūnosuke to take care, bade him farewell, and then walked on.

After the disaster, in the twilight, Ryūnosuke remained transfixed before the body of the Korean, the ground still rising and falling. And as Ryūnosuke stared at the body of the Korean, at all the bodies of the dead, as he stared across this city of rubble, across this city of smoke, everywhere he saw gears and wheels, translucent against the earth, against the sky, turning and spinning, grinding and screaming.

Four crows landed on adjacent poles. They stared first at the corpse, then at Ryūnosuke. Ryūnosuke took off his helmet. Ryūnosuke bowed his head. The biggest crow lifted its bloody beak heavenward and cawed

once, twice, a third time

and a fourth.

After the disaster, the official record stated that the Great Kantō Earthquake had had a magnitude of 7.9 on the Richter scale, that it had started at 11:58 a.m. on Saturday, September 1, 1923, and stopped after four minutes.

Ryūnosuke did not believe the official record. Ryūnosuke believed the earthquake would never stop. He believed the disaster was still to come.

Author's note: this work would not have been possible without the translations and scholarship of Edward Seidensticker, Donald Keene, Donald Richie, Howard Hibbett, G. H. Healey, Geoffrey Bownas, Beongcheon Yu, Seiji M. Lippit, and Jay Rubin. Its faults, though, remain mine.

—*David Peace*
Tokyo, 2011

AUTHORS

Kazushige Abe, born in 1968, was assistant director of several films before turning his energies to writing. He soon received recognition with a range of awards, including the Akutagawa Prize for *Grande Finale.*

Tetsuya Akikawa is an author, poet, and clown. His many novels and story collections include *Johnson the Crow* and *The Restaurant of Good Fortune.* He recently starred in the film *Hanezu,* directed by Naomi Kawase, which premiered at the 64th Cannes Film Festival in May 2011.

Hideo Furukawa, born in 1966, has won the Japan Mystery Writers Award, the Japan SF Award, and the Yukio Mishima Prize. His novel *Belka, Why Don't You Bark?* is currently being translated into English. He is a native of Fukushima.

Natsuki Ikezawa was born in 1945. He is a writer, critic, and translator who travels widely and has lived in France and Greece. His novels often address politics, nature, and the extension of economic might. *Still Lives* and *A Burden of Flowers* have been translated into English.

Shinji Ishii, born in 1966, is known for what critics have called "children's stories for adults." English translations of his short stories have appeared in several venues. He is editor of the Words & Bonds project in Japan, which emerged after the March 11 catastrophe.

Mitsuyo Kakuta began a promising career writing young adult fiction before concentrating on issues facing contemporary women in Japanese society. Born in 1967, she has two novels translated into English—*Woman on the Other Shore* and *The Eighth Day.*

Hiromi Kawakami, born in 1958, taught biology in high school before her short story "Kami-sama," which is translated here, won her the first of several significant awards. *Manazuru,* translated by Michael Emmerich, was recipient of the Japan-U.S. Friendship Commission Prize.

Mieko Kawakami is a novelist, poet, musician, and actress. She pursued a successful singing career before her short story "Myself and a Toothache" brought her wide critical attention. The following year her novel *Breast and Ovum* was awarded the Akutagawa Prize. She was born in 1976.

J. D. McClatchy, born in 1945, is a poet, critic, editor, opera librettist, and professor of literature. Currently editor of *The*

Yale Review, he is president of the American Academy of Arts and Letters.

Ryu Murakami's first novel, *Almost Transparent Blue,* published while he was an art student, was awarded the Akutagawa Prize and went on to sell over a million copies. Many of his novels have been translated into English, and he also hosts a TV talk show. He was born in 1952.

Brother & Sister Nishioka (known as Nishioka Kyodai) are actual siblings who have attracted a cult following for their literary manga, which they write and draw as a team. "A Country Doctor," based on Franz Kafka's short story, has been translated into English and published in *Monkey Business.*

Yoko Ogawa, born in 1962, has published more than twenty works of fiction and nonfiction, winning every major Japanese literary award. Her work has been translated into twenty-five languages, and English translations of her short stories and novels are widely available. *Hotel Iris,* translated by Stephen Snyder, was short-listed for the Man Asian Literary Prize.

David Peace was born in Yorkshire, England, in 1967. He is the author of the Red Riding Quartet, *GB84,* which was awarded the James Tait Black Memorial Prize, *The Damned Utd, Tokyo Year Zero,* and *Occupied City.* He was chosen as one of Granta's Best of Young British Novelists in 2003 and *GQ* Writer of the Year in 2007. He has lived in Japan since 1994.

Kazumi Saeki, born in 1959, was an electrician in Tokyo until he came down with asbestos poisoning, whereupon he moved back to his hometown, Sendai, and began to write. He moved to Norway for a year, producing the novel *Norge*, which was awarded the Noma Literary Prize.

John Burnham Schwartz is the author of *The Commoner, Claire Marvel, Bicycle Days, Reservation Road,* and *Northwest Corner.* A graduate in East Asian Studies at Harvard University, he has taught at the Iowa Writers' Workshop, Harvard, and Sarah Lawrence College, was recipient of the Lyndhurst Foundation Award for mastery in the art of fiction, and is currently literary director of the Sun Valley Writers' Conference. He lives in Brooklyn, New York.

Kiyoshi Shigematsu, born in 1963, worked as an editor before turning to writing. His breakthrough was the novel *Eiji*, based on a real-life murder of a sixth grader by a fourteen-year-old middle school student, which won him two literary awards.

Shuntaro Tanikawa, born in 1931, has written more than sixty books of poetry. Several collections have been translated into English, including *Floating the River in Melancholy,* by William I. Eliot and Kazuo Kawamura, which won the American Book Award in 1989.

Yoko Tawada, born in 1960, has won the Akutagawa Prize, the Tanizaki Prize, and the Ito Sei Award. Having moved to Germany at age twenty-two, she writes in both Japanese and German. She was awarded the Goethe Medal in 2005. *The Bridegroom Was a Dog,* translated by Margaret Mitsutani, and *Where Europe Begins,* translated by Susan Bernofsky and Yumi Selden, have been published in English.

Barry Yourgrau is a short-story writer, performer, and cell phone–fiction author, with a following at least as large in Japan, where he is translated by Motoyuki Shibata, as in the U.S. His books include *Wearing Dad's Head* and *The Sadness of Sex*, in whose film version he starred. He is working on a memoir entitled *Mess*. Born in South Africa, he lives in New York.

TRANSLATORS

Jeffrey Angles is Associate Professor of Japanese Literature and Translation Studies at Western Michigan University. He has translated short stories and memoirs as well as poetry, working with Hiromi Ito and Takako Arai. His translation of the poetry of Chimako Tada received the Japan-U.S. Friendship Commission Prize and the Harold Morton Landon Translation Award from the Academy of American Poets.

Alfred Birnbaum, who has lived in Japan more than thirty years, is a writer as well as a translator of art criticism, architecture, design, and contemporary fiction, including novels and short stories by Haruki Murakami, Miyuki Miyabe, and Natsuki Ikezawa. *Smile as They Bow,* by the Burmese writer Nu Nu Yi Inwa, which Birnbaum translated with his wife, Thi Thi Aye, was short-listed for the Man Asian Literary Prize.

Bonnie Elliott was born to a Japanese mother and Irish-American father in Zushi, Japan, and splits both heart and mind equally between the two cultures. She lives in Brooklyn, New York, and has published translations of short stories by Shinji Ishii.

Michael Emmerich is Assistant Professor of Japanese Literature and Cultural Studies at the University of California Santa Barbara. He has published widely in English and Japanese on early modern, modern, and contemporary Japanese literature, and has translated works by Yasunari Kawabata, Banana Yoshimoto, Gen'ichiro Takahashi, Mari Akasaka, Taichi Yamada, Rieko Matsuura, and Hiromi Kawakami. He is editor of *Read Real Japanese: Fiction* and *New Penguin Parallel Text: Short Stories in Japanese.*

Ted Goossen teaches at York University in Toronto, and is also affiliated with the Department of Contemporary Literary Studies at the University of Tokyo. He is the general editor of *The Oxford Book of Japanese Short Stories* and has published translations of stories and essays by Haruki Murakami, Naoya Shiga, Masuji Ibuse, and Ton Satomi, among others.

Jeffrey Hunter has worked as a translator and editor, specializing in religion, philosophy, art, architecture, and both modern and Edo-period literature. Among his translations are *Snow Country Tales (Hokuetsu Seppu)*, by Bokushi Suzuki; *Ando Shoeki: Collected Writings; Tariki: Embracing Despair, Discovering Peace,* by Hiroyuki Itsuki; short stories by Kyoji Kobayashi and Yoshinori Shimizu; *Tokyo Seven Roses,* by Hisashi Inoue;

and *Lost Souls and Sacred Monsters,* by Juko Nishimura. He lives in San Francisco.

Wayne P. Lammers is a freelance translator of literary and cultural texts. In 2007 his translation of *Woman on the Other Shore* introduced Mitsuyo Kakuta to the English-reading world. Besides contemporary fiction, his work has included a classical romance, memoirs, stage plays, screenplays and subtitles, manga, and a manga-based grammar guide, *Japanese the Manga Way.* He lives outside Portland, Oregon.

Ralph McCarthy's most recent translations are *Otogizoshi: The Fairy Tale Book of Dazai Osamu; Infinity Net: The Autobiography of Yayoi Kusama;* and *Popular Hits of the Showa Era,* by Ryu Murakami. He lives in Santa Monica, California.

Margaret Mitsutani is a translator and a teacher of modern literature and women's studies at Kyoritsu Women's University in Tokyo. Her translations include *An Echo of Heaven* by Kenzaburo Oe and *The Bridegroom Was a Dog* by Yoko Tawada.

Motoyuki Shibata, who teaches at the University of Tokyo, is an essayist and translator of American literature. Among writers he has translated are Paul Auster, Steven Millhauser, Stuart Dybek, Richard Powers, Philip Roth, and Thomas Pynchon. He received the Kodansha Essay Prize for *A Half-Baked Scholar* (Nama Hanka na Gakusha) and the Suntory Humanities Prize for *American Narcissus.* He is also editor of the literary magazine *Monkey Business* (published in both Japanese and English versions).

Stephen Snyder is Kawashima Professor of Japanese Studies at Middlebury College in Vermont. He is the author of *Fictions of Desire: Narrative Form in the Novels of Nagai Kafu* and coeditor of *Oe and Beyond: Fiction in Contemporary Japan.* He has translated works by Yoko Ogawa, Kenzaburo Oe, Ryu Murakami, Miri Yu, and Natsuo Kirino, among others. His translation of Kunio Tsuji's *Azuchi Okanki* (The Signore) was awarded the 1990 Japan-U.S. Friendship Commission Prize.